THE
PURPOSE
AND POWER
OF THE BELIEVER
ON EARTH

Discovering and Living the Life
God Designed for You

TOM CORNELL

THE PURPOSE AND POWER OF THE BELIEVER ON EARTH

DISCOVERING AND LIVING THE LIFE GOD DESIGNED FOR YOU

TOM CORNELL

SOZO PUBLISHING

CONTENTS

INTRODUCTION
MORE THAN WAITING FOR HEAVEN

A lot of believers love the Lord but live what I call a boring Christian life. They genuinely believe, they go to church, they know they're saved—but deep down they live as though Christianity is only about holding on until heaven. For them, the Christian life becomes reduced to a single moment at the altar and then a long waiting game until the rapture or until their time on earth is done.

But here's the problem: if God's whole intent was simply to get you to heaven, the second you gave your life to Christ, He would have taken you home. The fact that you are still here is proof that He has a greater purpose. And because so many believers never understand that purpose, they live beneath the life God intended. They never step into the joy, the adventure, and the power of what it really means to be a Spirit-filled son or daughter of God on the earth.

That is why this book matters. Its intent is to open your eyes through the Scriptures to the true purpose of the believer's life on earth—and to show you that it is anything but boring. You were never meant to limp through life waiting for heaven. You were created to release heaven on earth. God is not just trying to get you into heaven; He is trying to get heaven into you, and then through you, into the world around you.

This is not theory—it is the real Christian life. And once you begin to understand it, everything changes. Life with God becomes exciting, adventurous, and full of power. Heaven begins to invade the earth through your ordinary, everyday moments. Prayers carry authority. Homes become greenhouses of God's presence. Cities feel the weight of God's kingdom breaking in. And believers stop talking only about "one day" in heaven and begin to live like the kingdom is already here— because it is.

I remember when this shift happened for me. My home changed. It went from being just a house to becoming a greenhouse of the kingdom. The atmosphere shifted. My children began to expect answers when we prayed. Friends who didn't even know the Lord would walk in and ask, "Why does it feel different here?" It wasn't personality or décor. It was the Presence. Heaven had touched earth in an ordinary living room. And I realized: this is the life God intends for every believer— not someday, but now.

That's the journey I want to invite you into. Here's what you will discover in the chapters ahead:

- Part I reveals the kingdom Jesus inaugurated: the "now and not yet" reality that reframes how we live.
- Part II unpacks the twofold work of the Holy Spirit —in you for transformation and upon you for power.

- Part III shows you how to host God's presence in daily life—your home, your habits, your relationships, your purity.
- Part IV calls you to demonstration: healing the sick, casting out darkness, prophesying, praying in tongues, walking in boldness, and making disciples.

Along the way, you'll find practical tools and activations: Scripture confessions, prayer guides, consecration practices for your home, ministry quick-cards, and even a 30-day "Open-Heaven Activation Plan" to help you practice what you're learning.

If you take these truths to heart, this book won't just inspire you—it will transform you. You'll step out of the "boring Christian life" and into the vibrant, Spirit-filled adventure God intended. The heavens are already open. The Spirit has already been given. And your Father is waiting to delight you with His kingdom.

It's time to stop waiting for heaven. It's time to start living as heaven touches earth—through your life.

PART ONE
THE KINGDOM NOW AND NOT YET

CHAPTER 1
YOUR FATHER'S GOOD PLEASURE

J esus once spoke words to His disciples that reveal the very heart of God for His children: *"Do not be afraid, little flock, for it is your Father's good pleasure to give you the kingdom."* (Luke 12:32 NKJV)

What a picture of the Father's heart! He is not reluctant. He does not hesitate. He is not dangling promises in front of us like a cruel game of keep-away. He delights—He takes pleasure—in giving His children His kingdom. That means the kingdom of God is not something you have to fight for, climb toward, or beg to receive. It is a gift given by a Father who loves you.

Too often we imagine God as a stern judge or distant ruler, withholding His presence until we've proven ourselves worthy. But Jesus shatters that image with a single phrase: "It is your Father's pleasure to give you the kingdom." The kingdom is not earned—it's inherited. It is received by sons and daughters who know their Father's heart.

The Kingdom Defined

But what exactly is the kingdom of God?

The kingdom is not primarily a place—it is a reign. It is the domain of God, the sphere where His will is perfectly done. The kingdom has to do with the King, His reign, and His rule.

Wherever God's authority is acknowledged and His will is embraced, the kingdom is manifest. In heaven, this is already a present reality. Heaven is the environment where God's rule is absolute, His purposes are unhindered, and His presence fills everything. That is why there is no sickness, no fear, no rebellion, and no oppression in heaven.

When Jesus came preaching the gospel of the kingdom, He was declaring that God's reign was breaking into the world. Every healing, every deliverance, every forgiven sinner, every broken life restored was a sign that heaven's government was invading earth's disorder. That's why He taught His disciples to pray, *"Your kingdom come, Your will be done, on earth as it is in heaven."(Matthew 6:10 NKJV)*

That prayer is not a poetic flourish or a religious formula. It is a command. It is an invitation to align our lives with God's original design and to see His reign made visible in our homes, our workplaces, our cities, and our nations. When we pray this way, we are saying: "Father, let earth look like heaven. Let my life come into alignment with what You always intended."

The Father's Pleasure

Think again about Jesus' words in Luke 12. He didn't just say the kingdom is available—He said the Father takes pleasure in giving it. That word is crucial. The kingdom is not reluctantly given but joyfully bestowed. God is not reluctant to bless His children; it is His delight.

This means the starting point for kingdom life is not striving but receiving. Sons and daughters don't beg for their inheritance—they receive it with confidence, knowing it comes from a generous Father. This changes everything. When you understand that the kingdom is given in delight, not withheld in suspicion, you can live from rest instead of striving, from faith instead of fear.

Fear is one of the greatest enemies of kingdom living. Fear convinces you that God is withholding, that you are disqualified, that you don't measure up. But Jesus says, "Do not be afraid." Why? Because your Father has already decided—He delights to give you the kingdom.

On Earth as It Is in Heaven

When Jesus instructed His disciples to pray *"on earth as it is in heaven" (Matt. 6:10),* He was revealing the heartbeat of the Father. Heaven is the place where God's will is done perfectly. To pray that heaven would come to earth is to ask that God's will would be done here with the same clarity, purity, and power as it is there.

This prayer is not just about the future. It is about today. Jesus was not telling us to dream about a someday kingdom. He was teaching us to call it into the present. Every time you pray, every time you obey, every time you act in faith—you create a landing strip for heaven to touch earth. Think about what that means:

- In heaven there is peace, so when His kingdom comes, chaos in your mind and home must bow.
- In heaven there is joy, so when His kingdom comes, despair and depression are displaced.
- In heaven there is wholeness, so when His kingdom comes, bodies are healed and lives are restored.
- In heaven there is holiness, so when His kingdom comes, purity and righteousness begin to shape culture.

"To live on earth as it is in heaven" means to live under the reign of the King here and now, allowing His perfect intent to manifest in your ordinary, everyday life.

Sons and Daughters of the Kingdom

Notice again the language Jesus uses: "Your Father's good pleasure." Not "the Judge's cold decree," not "the Master's reluctant nod." The kingdom is the Father's gift. That means you are not approaching Him as a stranger or a beggar—you are His child.

Sons and daughters don't earn inheritance; they receive it. Orphans, however, are never sure if they belong. They strive, they compete, they beg for scraps, they live insecure. Too many Christians live with an orphan mindset. They believe they have to convince God to bless them, to heal them, to use them. But Jesus is clear: the kingdom is the Father's pleasure to give.

When you live as a son or daughter, you begin to walk with confidence. You stop striving for approval and start living from identity. You no longer approach God wondering if He wants to give—you approach Him knowing it delights Him to pour out His kingdom on you.

A Rhythm of Prayer

So how do we practically live this out? One of the most powerful tools Jesus gave us is the Lord's Prayer (Matthew 6:9-11). But instead of reciting it quickly and moving on, we can use it as a rhythm for our daily lives.

- Adoration: *"Our Father in heaven, hallowed be Your name."* Begin by worshiping Him. Lift your heart in praise. See Him for who He is.
- Alignment: *"Your kingdom come, Your will be done, on earth as it is in heaven."* Lay down your agenda. Align your heart with His. Invite His rule into every area of your life.
- Assignment: *"Give us today our daily bread... forgive us... deliver us from evil."* Step into the day's assignment with provision, forgiveness, and protection.

This pattern—adoration, alignment, assignment—reshapes your posture toward God and trains you to live under His reign daily.

Reflection Questions

1. When you hear the word "kingdom," what have you thought it meant? How does the idea of the kingdom as God's reign and rule expand your understanding?
2. What does it mean to you that the Father delights to give you His kingdom?
3. Where in your life do you most need to pray, "on earth as it is in heaven"?
4. How might the Lord's Prayer become more of a daily rhythm than a religious recitation for you?
5. What orphan mindsets might still keep you from receiving the kingdom as a son or daughter?

Prayer

Father, thank You that Your kingdom is not distant or withheld, but joyfully given to me. I receive the truth that Your kingdom is Your reign and rule breaking into my life. I ask that Your will be done in me and through me as it is in heaven. Teach me to live as a son/daughter who receives and carries Your kingdom with confidence. Let heaven's peace, joy, and wholeness touch every part of my life. In Jesus' name, amen.

Declarations

- It is my Father's good pleasure to give me the kingdom.
- The kingdom is the reign and rule of God breaking into my life.
- I live under open heavens because of Jesus.
- My life is a landing strip for heaven on earth.
- I am not an orphan—I am a son/daughter, and I carry the kingdom with confidence.

CHAPTER 2

THE GREAT UNVEILING: RENDED HEAVENS, RENDED VEIL

There are cries in Scripture that echo through the centuries, prayers so deep they capture the longing of all creation. Isaiah uttered one of them: *"Oh, that You would rend the heavens and come down, that the mountains would tremble before You!"* (Isaiah 64:1 NIV).

To rend is not to gently open. It means to tear violently, to split apart. Isaiah was pleading for God to tear open the heavens, to remove the separation between heaven and earth, and to come down with His presence and power. It was the cry of a prophet who knew things were not as they were meant to be. Centuries later, that cry was answered.

The Baptism of Jesus: Heavens Torn Open

When Jesus stepped into the Jordan River, the ordinary became extraordinary. Mark describes the moment with unusual intensity: *"Just as Jesus was coming up out of the water, He saw heaven being torn open and the Spirit descending on Him like a dove."* (Mark 1:10 NIV).

The language is deliberate. The heavens were not politely

parted; they were torn. The same word Isaiah used is used here. The cry of the prophet became the reality of the Messiah.

Before this, Jesus lived in obscurity. He was sinless, filled with wisdom, and growing in favor with God and man, but we have no record of miracles. No blind eyes opened. No storms stilled. No demons cast out. Then the heavens were torn, the Spirit descended, and everything shifted. Jesus began to move in power because heaven had broken into earth in a new way.

This was not just a personal empowerment for Jesus; it was a prophetic sign for us. In Him, the heavens are permanently open. What descended upon Him was not meant to lift but to remain — and to be shared with His body, the Church.

The Cross: Veil Torn in Two

Fast-forward to the final moments of Jesus' earthly ministry. As He gave up His spirit on the cross, Matthew records: *"At that moment the curtain of the temple was torn in two from top to bottom. The earth shook, the rocks split and the tombs broke open. The bodies of many holy people who had died were raised to life."* (Matthew 27:51–52 NIV).

Again, something is torn. This time it's not the heavens but the veil in the temple. That curtain, some 60 feet high and impossibly thick, separated the Most Holy Place — the dwelling of God's presence — from everyone else. Only the high priest, once a year, could pass beyond it with sacrificial blood. The veil represented distance, separation, barriers.

But at the cross, the separation ended. The veil was torn not from bottom to top, as if by human effort, but from top to bottom — the hand of God Himself. His presence was no longer locked away. His Spirit was no longer hidden. The way was now open for every believer to live in His presence.

And notice the signs that followed: the earth shook, rocks split, tombs opened, and dead people rose. When barriers are torn down, resurrection life breaks out. What Isaiah longed for had come to pass: heaven and earth colliding, God's presence invading, death losing its grip.

Eden: Where It All Began

To understand the tearing of the heavens and the tearing of the veil, we need to go back to the beginning. In Eden, heaven and earth were not separate realms. They overlapped. God walked with Adam and Eve in the cool of the day. His space and our space were one. Humanity was created to live in unbroken fellowship with the Creator, stewarding creation as God's image-bearers.

But sin fractured this unity. Adam and Eve were expelled from the garden, and a flaming sword was placed at the entrance — a barrier between God's presence and humanity. What was once natural became impossible. Heaven and earth were no longer one; they were divided.

Tabernacle and Temple: Temporary Overlaps

Even in separation, God still desired to dwell with His people. So He instructed Moses to build a tabernacle — a tent of meeting — where His presence could rest in the midst of Israel's camp. Later, Solomon built a temple, a permanent structure where God's glory would dwell.

But both were temporary solutions. God's presence was

real, but it was limited. Only the high priest could enter the Most Holy Place. God's dwelling was in a building made by human hands, not in the hearts of His people. It was never His ultimate intent.

That's why, when David desired to build a house for God, the Lord responded, *"Would you build me a house to dwell in? Did I ever ask for one?"* (2 Samuel 7:5–7 NIV). God was hinting at something greater. He never desired to live in stone or wood; He longed to dwell in living temples.

Christ: The True Tabernacle

This longing found its fulfillment in Jesus. John 1:14 says, *"The Word became flesh and made His dwelling among us."* The Greek word there is literally "tabernacled." Jesus was the walking, breathing tabernacle of God — God's presence in human flesh. Where He went, heaven broke in. Where He spoke, God's reign was established. Where He touched, sickness and oppression fled.

Jesus was not just carrying the Spirit for Himself; He was modeling what it would look like for God's presence to dwell with His people again.

Believers: Living Temples

When the veil was torn at the cross, access was granted not just for us to enter God's presence but for His presence to enter us. Paul writes, *"Do you not know that you are God's temple and that God's Spirit dwells in you?"* (1 Corinthians 3:16 ESV).

This is breathtaking. God does not live in tents or temples

anymore. He lives in you. You are the tabernacle of God. You are the place where heaven and earth overlap.

This means that wherever you go, you carry an open heaven. Your workplace, your neighborhood, your home can all become environments where God's presence is revealed because you are there. You are not waiting for God to show up; He has already shown up in you.

Revelation 21: The New Eden

The story comes full circle in Revelation 21. John describes the new heaven and new earth, the holy city coming down, and declares: *"And I heard a loud voice from the throne saying, 'Now the dwelling of God is with men, and He will live with them. They will be His people, and God Himself will be with them and be their God.'"* *(Revelation 21:3 NIV).*

Notice what is missing: a temple. John writes, *"I did not see a temple in the city, because the Lord God Almighty and the Lamb are its temple." (Revelation 21:22 NIV).* Why? Because there is no longer any separation. Heaven and earth are one again. God's dwelling with humanity is complete. The new Jerusalem is the new Eden, a restored creation where everything broken has been made whole.

This is God's intent from the beginning — not escape, but union. Not distance, but dwelling. The torn heavens and the torn veil were not isolated events; they were signs pointing to God's ultimate plan to unite heaven and earth in Christ.

Living Under an Open Heaven

So what does this mean for us now? It means you no longer

live under separation. You live under an open heaven. You are a dwelling place of God. You are a living temple. And you are called to manifest heaven on earth in your daily life.

When you worship, you are not trying to reach a God who is far off; you are communing with the One who dwells in you. When you pray, you are not begging for a closed heaven to open; you are aligning with the reality that it already is. When you minister, you are not asking for power to fall; you are releasing the power that rests upon you.

Isaiah's cry has been answered. The heavens are open. The veil is torn. The Spirit has been given. Now it is our turn to live as living temples, carriers of His presence, advancing the overlap of heaven and earth until the day when the whole earth becomes the new Eden.

Reflection Questions

1. How does the picture of Eden as heaven and earth overlapping reshape the way you see God's intent for creation?
2. What does it mean to you personally that the heavens are already open and the veil is already torn?
3. In what ways do you still live as if God is distant or His presence is locked away?
4. How can you cultivate the awareness that you are God's temple and a dwelling place of His Spirit?
5. Where in your life do you long to see heaven and earth overlap more fully?

Prayer

Father, thank You that from the very beginning Your desire was to dwell with Your people. Thank You that in Christ the heavens are open and the veil is torn. I repent for living as if You were distant, when You are near. Teach me to live as Your temple, aware of Your presence within me and upon me. Let my life be a place where heaven and earth meet. Use me to bring Your presence into my family, my workplace, and my city. Until the day You dwell fully with Your people in the new Eden, let me be a faithful carrier of Your presence here and now. In Jesus' name, amen.

Declarations

- The heavens are open because of Jesus.
- The veil is torn; I have full access to God's presence.
- I am a living temple, the dwelling place of God's Spirit.
- Heaven and earth overlap in my life.
- I live under an open heaven and release God's presence wherever I go.

CHAPTER 3

ROYAL SEARCH: KINGS WHO SEEK MYSTERIES

There is a beautiful tension in the Kingdom of God. On one hand, God delights to give His kingdom to His children. On the other, He conceals treasures in such a way that only the hungry will discover them. This is not contradiction—it is invitation.

> Proverbs 25:2 says: *"It is the glory of God to conceal a matter; to search out a matter is the glory of kings." NKJV*

This is not a random proverb. It is a window into how the kingdom operates. God's glory is revealed in His ability to hide treasures. Our glory, as sons and daughters who have been made royalty, is revealed when we seek those treasures out.

This means you are not just a passive recipient in the kingdom of God. You are an active participant. God has hidden mysteries—not from you, but for you. He has concealed truths in Scripture, wisdom in His Spirit, strategies for your life and destiny, and even breakthroughs for your city, waiting for you to seek them out.

You Are Royalty

Before we go further, you need to be reminded of your identity. Proverbs says it is the glory of kings to search things out. Who are those kings? In Christ, you are.

Revelation 1:6 tells us that Jesus has made us *"kings and priests to our God."* 1 Peter 2:9 declares that we are a *"royal priesthood."* Sons and daughters of the King of kings carry royal bloodline.

Royalty has access that commoners don't. Royalty has responsibility to steward what is found. You are not meant to live as a spiritual beggar, hoping for scraps of revelation. You are invited into the throne room, given access to the King's heart, and called to search out the mysteries of His kingdom.

Searching is not for the spiritually elite. It is the privilege of every son and daughter.

Hidden but Not Withheld

If God delights to give us the kingdom (Luke 12:32), why does He conceal things? Isn't that unfair?

Think about it this way: parents often hide Easter eggs for their children, not to withhold candy but to create the joy of discovery. The hunt itself creates excitement, teaches persistence, and makes the finding all the more meaningful. The reward is sweeter because of the search.

God is a Father who delights to watch His children discover. When you dig into Scripture and suddenly a verse comes alive, He smiles. When you sit in prayer and the Spirit whispers something you've never seen before, heaven rejoices. When you press in for answers and revelation breaks through, your Father delights.

Mysteries are not meant to keep you out; they are meant to draw you in.

The Keys of the Kingdom

Jesus took this even further when He told His disciples: *"I will give you the keys of the kingdom of heaven; whatever you bind on earth will be bound in heaven, and whatever you loose on earth will be loosed in heaven." (Matthew 16:19 NIV)*.

Keys unlock doors. Keys release access. Keys represent authority. The keys of the kingdom are the mysteries of how heaven operates.

When you discover a key, you discover a way that heaven moves. You discover how God's government works. That key gives you authority to unlock heaven's resources and release them on earth.

Think of forgiveness as a key. Jesus said if you forgive, you will be forgiven (Matthew 6:14). That's not just a nice principle —it's a kingdom law. It's a way heaven operates. When you apply that key in your relationships, you are walking in agreement with heaven, and heaven is released through your life.

This is why searching matters. Kings search because keys are hidden. The mysteries of the kingdom are the keys of the kingdom. They are not lying on the surface for the casual passerby. They are concealed for the hungry, for those who honor the King enough to dig.

Walking in Agreement

The prophet Amos wrote, *"Can two walk together unless they are agreed?" (Amos 3:3 NKJV)*. The answer is no. Agreement is necessary for partnership.

This principle applies to our walk with God. God is not going to change His mind to walk with us. He is holy. He is truth. He is perfect. He cannot lie, compromise, or lower Himself to our ways. If we are going to walk with Him, we must change our minds. We must repent—literally "change the way we think"—and come into agreement with His ways.

That's what the keys of the kingdom are: the ways of the kingdom. To use a key is to honor a way. To honor a way is to agree with the King. And when you agree with Him, you walk with Him, and heaven is released through your life.

Agreement is not passive—it requires alignment. The royal search is not about information; it's about transformation. When you discover a key, you are responsible to use it. Revelation demands response.

The Torah and the Way

This idea of God's ways goes all the way back to the Old Testament. Israel was given the Law of Moses. In Hebrew, the word for law is Torah. Torah doesn't just mean law in the sense of rules; it means "the way."

The Torah revealed the way God's kingdom operates. It was a pattern, a shadow pointing forward. By following the Torah, Israel learned how to walk with God, how to host His presence, how to live in alignment with His ways.

But here is the stunning reality: Jesus came as the Torah made flesh.

John 1:14 says, *"The Word became flesh and dwelt among us."* The Greek literally says He "tabernacled" among us. Heaven invaded earth through Jesus, because He is the Way. He is the Torah, the Word, the blueprint of heaven's operation, embodied.

When Jesus said, *"I am the way, the truth, and the life"* (John 14:6 NKJV), He was saying, "I am the Torah fulfilled. I am the way of heaven embodied. Walk with Me, and you will walk in agreement with the Father."

That's why He could give us the keys of the kingdom—because He Himself is the way of the kingdom.

Secrets for Those Who Fear Him

Psalm 25:14 declares: *"The secret of the Lord is with those who fear Him, and He will show them His covenant." NKJV*

God does not share His secrets with the casual or the careless. He shares them with those who fear Him—with those who honor, revere, and treasure His presence.

Think about it: you don't share your deepest secrets with everyone. You share them with those closest to you, those you trust. In the same way, God reserves His mysteries for those who love Him deeply, who honor Him with their lives, who are willing to walk in His ways.

Royal searching requires holy fear. It requires reverence. It requires the humility to say, "God, I don't know, but You do.

Teach me Your ways."

The Spirit Who Searches

Paul picks up this theme in 1 Corinthians 2. He writes:

"No eye has seen, no ear has heard, no mind has conceived what God has prepared for those who love him"—but God has revealed it to us by His Spirit. The Spirit searches all things, even the deep things of God." (1 Corinthians 2:9–10 NIV)

This is stunning. The Spirit of God is not only present to comfort you or empower you—He is actively searching the depths of God. And He dwells in you. That means you have access to mysteries hidden in God's heart that no natural wisdom could uncover.

Paul continues: *"We have received… the Spirit who is from God, that we may understand what God has freely given us." (v. 12).*

Do you see the connection? Proverbs says kings search out mysteries. Paul says the Spirit searches the deep things of God. Put them together, and you realize: your royal search is empowered by the Spirit's search. You are not left to figure it out alone. The same Spirit who searches God's depths reveals those things to you.

That's why Paul concludes the chapter with this audacious statement: *"But we have the mind of Christ." (v. 16).*

The Spirit who searches God's heart gives you access to the very mind of Christ. You don't just guess at mysteries; you are invited to think His thoughts after Him.

Searching with Scripture

So where do we begin our royal search? Always with Scripture. The Word of God is not just information; it is revelation. It is living and active, sharper than any double-edged sword (Hebrews 4:12). It is Spirit-breathed, carrying the wisdom and heart of God.

Every page of your Bible contains treasure. Every verse is an entry point into encounter. But here's the difference between casual reading and royal searching: hunger.

Casual reading skims. Royal searching lingers. Casual reading collects facts. Royal searching seeks transformation. Casual reading looks for what is obvious. Royal searching presses in for what is hidden.

Jesus Himself modeled this. After His resurrection, He walked with two disciples on the road to Emmaus and "opened the Scriptures" to them, showing how everything pointed to Him (Luke 24:27). Their hearts burned because He revealed mysteries hidden in plain sight.

That same Spirit walks with you when you open your Bible.

The "Scripture Listening" Method

Here's a simple way to search the Scriptures with the Spirit's help:

1. Read Slowly. Don't rush. Take a small portion of Scripture—maybe a verse or two. Read it aloud. Pause. Read it again.

2. Ask Questions. What stands out? Why this word? Why this phrase? What's the context? Write down questions, even if you don't yet have answers.
3. Listen for the Spirit. Invite the Holy Spirit: "Search the deep things of God and reveal them to me." Wait in silence. Pay attention to impressions, thoughts, or highlights.
4. Cross-Reference. Let Scripture interpret Scripture. If a word or phrase stands out, trace it through other parts of the Bible.
5. Write and Pray. Journal what you sense. Turn it into prayer. Thank God for what He revealed and ask Him how to apply it.

This is not about mastering information. It's about letting the Word master you. It's about encountering the Author in the text.

Royal Responsibility

When you discover a mystery, you also receive responsibility. Royalty doesn't hoard treasures—it stewards them. God reveals things not just for your benefit but for the benefit of others.

Think of Joseph in Egypt. God gave him dreams and the interpretation of Pharaoh's dream. That revelation was not just for Joseph's personal encouragement. It was a strategy to save nations from famine. Revelation carried responsibility.

In the same way, when God reveals something to you, ask: "Who is this for? How should I steward this?" Sometimes it is personal encouragement. Sometimes it is for intercession. Sometimes it is a word to share with someone else. Sometimes it is a strategy for your business, your church, or your family. Mysteries are meant to be multiplied, not buried.

Obstacles to the Royal Search

Why don't more believers experience this kind of discovery? Often it's because of one of these obstacles:

1. Passivity. Some Christians don't search because they don't believe there's more to find. They settle for surface-level faith.
2. Fear. Others are afraid of being deceived. They fear seeking deeper things will lead them astray. But when you anchor in Scripture and the Spirit, God knows how to keep you safe.
3. Hurry. Many simply don't slow down long enough. Revelation often comes in stillness, not busyness.
4. Pride. Some approach Scripture to prove themselves right, not to be transformed. Pride blinds us to mystery.

The good news? Each of these obstacles can be overcome with humility, hunger, and the help of the Spirit.

Practicing the Royal Search

Let me give you a challenge: pick one passage this week and practice Scripture listening. Don't rush through a chapter. Choose just a few verses. Sit with them. Ask the Spirit to show you what is hidden. Journal what you hear.

And don't be surprised if something you discover becomes fuel for encouragement in someone else's life. That's how the kingdom works. What God reveals to you often becomes a gift for those around you.

Reflection Questions

1. How does Proverbs 25:2 reshape the way you view mysteries in the kingdom?
2. What does it mean to you that God hides things for you, not from you?
3. How do the keys of the kingdom help you walk in agreement with God?
4. Where do you need to realign your thinking so you can walk with Him?
5. Have you ever experienced God sharing a "secret" with you as you searched His Word or sought His presence? What did you do with it?

Prayer

Father, thank You that You are a God who hides treasures, not to withhold them, but to invite us into the joy of discovery. Thank You for giving me the keys of the kingdom. Teach me to search Your Word with hunger, to honor Your ways, and to walk in agreement with You. Jesus, You are the Way—the Torah made flesh. Let my life come into full alignment with You. Holy Spirit, search the deep things of God and reveal them to me. And may every revelation I receive bear fruit for others. In Jesus' name, amen.

Declarations

- I am royalty in Christ, invited to search out the mysteries of God.
- God hides treasures for me, not from me.
- The keys of the kingdom are mine to discover and use.
- I walk in agreement with God by honoring His ways.
- Jesus is the Way, the Torah made flesh, and I walk with Him.
- What God reveals to me, I will steward with honor and release for others.

PART TWO
IN & UPON: THE TWOFOLD
WORK OF THE HOLY SPIRIT

CHAPTER 4
THE SPIRIT WITHIN: FORMATION & FRUIT

When you said yes to Jesus, more happened than a change of label from "sinner" to "saved." Something supernatural took place inside of you. Ezekiel 36:26–27* records God's promise:

> *"I will give you a new heart and put a new spirit in you; I will remove from you your heart of stone and give you a heart of flesh. And I will put my Spirit in you and move you to follow my decrees and be careful to keep my laws."*

This is not poetry. It is reality. When you were born again, God did not just polish your old heart—He replaced it. He took out the stone, unfeeling and resistant, and gave you a new heart responsive to Him. He put His Spirit within you, causing you to want what He wants.

The Spirit within is God's first great gift to every believer. It is the foundation of intimacy, the source of holiness, and the soil from which kingdom fruit grows.

---

* NIV

From Stone to Flesh

A heart of stone is hard, cold, and unresponsive. It resists the touch of God. It may know rules but has no power to live them. Many people live with stony hearts—numb to God, calloused toward people, trapped in cycles of sin.

But when you believed, God gave you a heart of flesh. Flesh here doesn't mean sinful nature—it means softness, tenderness, responsiveness. A new heart that beats with His desires, that feels His presence, that longs for His ways.

This is why Christianity is not primarily about external law but about internal transformation. The Spirit within changes what you want. Things you once craved now grieve you. Things you once resisted now draw you. You discover new desires—desires for holiness, for purity, for His Word, for His presence.

Desire Is the First Fruit

Desire is the first evidence of the Spirit within. The fact that you hunger for God, that you want His ways, that you long for His presence—that itself is proof of His Spirit inside of you.

The enemy will try to condemn you for not being "holy enough." But the very hunger you feel is evidence of new birth. Stone hearts don't hunger. Flesh hearts do. Don't despise hunger. Feed it.

This is why intimacy is possible. The Spirit within awakens your desires so you can draw near to God. You can love Him not just because you are told to, but because you want to. That want is His work in you.

The Fruit of the Spirit

Paul gives us the clearest picture of the Spirit within in Galatians 5:22–23 NIV:

"But the fruit of the Spirit is love, joy, peace, forbearance, kindness, goodness, faithfulness, gentleness and self-control. Against such things there is no law."

Notice it is "fruit," not "fruits." These nine qualities are not separate items you pick from a list. They are facets of one fruit —the life of the Spirit within you.

Fruit is not manufactured; it is produced. Apple trees don't strain to bear apples. They simply remain rooted, and fruit comes naturally. In the same way, when you remain rooted in Christ, the Spirit within you produces kingdom culture in your character.

Love—sacrificial, unconditional.
Joy—overflowing gladness not dependent on circumstances.
Peace—wholeness, rest, stability in the storm.
Patience—long-suffering, enduring without giving up.
Kindness—gentle strength that heals and uplifts.
Goodness—moral integrity, wholeness of life.
Faithfulness—dependability rooted in trust in God.
Gentleness—strength under control.
Self-control—mastery of desires and appetites.

This is kingdom culture growing in you. It is what heaven looks like in character form.

Formation Before Demonstration

The Spirit within always precedes the Spirit upon. In other words, God forms before He empowers. Before you walk in miracles, He wants you to walk in holiness. Before you shake nations, He wants you rooted in intimacy.

Why? Because power without character is dangerous. If you prophesy without love, Paul says you are just a noisy gong (1 Corinthians 13). If you heal the sick but have no self-control, you may draw crowds but you won't carry the kingdom.

The Spirit within forms you into someone who can be trusted with the Spirit upon. It is the foundation. Fruit must precede gifts. Formation must precede demonstration.

The Spirit and the Way

Here's where the connection to the "keys of the kingdom" becomes clear. The Spirit within doesn't just give you feelings —it trains you in God's ways.

Remember: the kingdom operates by ways. God doesn't change His mind to walk with us—we must change our minds to walk with Him. The Spirit within makes that possible. He shifts our desires so that we begin to love God's ways, to honor His keys, to come into agreement.

In the Old Testament, Torah was the way. In the New Testament, Jesus is the Way. And now, by His Spirit, the Way is written on your heart. You don't just know about it; you feel it. You want it. You are empowered to live it.

This is why Paul says in Romans 8:14 NIV: *"For those who are led by the Spirit of God are the children of God."* The Spirit within leads you into the ways of God. He forms you into someone who can walk with Him.

Intimacy: The Spirit as Comforter

Jesus promised in John 14 that the Spirit would come as Comforter. Comfort doesn't just mean consolation when you're sad. It means strength poured into you, presence alongside you.

The Spirit within whispers, reassures, guides. He reminds you that you are not an orphan but a son or daughter (Romans 8:15–16). This intimacy is the foundation of Christian life. You don't serve a distant God. You walk with a God who lives inside you.

Prayer becomes dialogue. Worship becomes encounter. Scripture becomes conversation. The Spirit within makes intimacy normal.

Holiness: The Spirit as Convicter

The Spirit within is also Convicter. Jesus said in John 16:8 that the Spirit would convict the world of sin, righteousness, and judgment. Conviction is not condemnation. Conviction is clarity. It is the Spirit saying, *"This is not who you are anymore. Walk this way instead."*

When you sin, the Spirit within grieves—not to reject you but to call you higher. Holiness is not just avoiding sin; it is living aligned with God's nature. The Spirit within empowers that.

This is why Paul calls your body *"the temple of the Holy Spirit" (1 Corinthians 6:19 NKJV).* God does not dwell in temples made with hands—He dwells in you. And He will not share His temple with idols. The Spirit within empowers you to cleanse the temple, to live holy, to be set apart.

Fruit That Remains

Jesus said in John 15:16 NIV, *"I chose you and appointed you so that you might go and bear fruit—fruit that will last."*

The fruit of the Spirit is not temporary. It is eternal. Power may fade. Gifts may cease. But fruit remains. When you love, when you walk in peace, when you live with integrity—you are building something that echoes into eternity.

This is why God values formation so highly. What He does within you is eternal. What He does through you is powerful, but temporary compared to the eternal character He is forming inside.

Obstacles to Formation

Why don't more believers live from this inner reality? Often it is because of:

1. Neglect. Ignoring the Spirit's whispers.
2. Distraction. Filling life with noise, leaving no room for His voice.
3. Compromise. Tolerating sin that hardens the heart again.
4. Pride. Believing formation is unnecessary because of external success.

The solution is simple but not easy: abide. Abide in Christ.

Attend to the Spirit within. Keep your heart tender. Respond quickly when He convicts. Stay hungry.

Practicing Life with the Spirit Within

Here are three practices to cultivate fruit:

1. Daily Surrender. Each morning, pray: "Holy Spirit, write Your ways on my heart today. Lead me in Your desires."
2. Fruit Inventory. Regularly examine your life against Galatians 5:22–23. Where is fruit flourishing? Where is it lacking? Invite the Spirit to cultivate it.
3. Rule of Life. Establish rhythms that make space for the Spirit—Scripture, prayer, silence, community, rest. Fruit grows in rhythms.

Reflection Questions

1. What evidence do you see in your life that God has given you a new heart?
2. How has the Spirit within changed your desires since you came to Christ?
3. Which fruit of the Spirit is most evident in your life? Which needs more cultivation?
4. How do you respond when the Spirit convicts you? Do you see it as condemnation or invitation?
5. What rhythms can you establish to give space for the Spirit to form fruit in you?

Prayer

Holy Spirit, thank You for living within me. Thank You for giving me a new heart, tender and responsive. Thank You for awakening holy desires and empowering me to walk in God's ways. Cultivate Your fruit in me—love, joy, peace, patience, kindness, goodness, faithfulness, gentleness, and self-control. Conform me to the image of Christ. Keep me tender, responsive, and hungry for more of You. In Jesus' name, amen.

Declarations

- I have been given a new heart and a new spirit.
- The Spirit within me awakens holy desires.
- I am a temple of the Holy Spirit, set apart for God.
- The fruit of the Spirit is growing in me daily.
- I walk in God's ways because His Spirit writes them on my heart.
- My life bears fruit that remains for eternity.

CHAPTER 5

THE SPIRIT UPON: POWER & PURPOSE

The Spirit within is the miracle of new birth—God's own life planted in your heart, producing fruit, forming holiness, and awakening intimacy. But God never intended His Spirit to stop at the level of private transformation. The Spirit is also meant to rest upon you for the sake of the world.

Jesus Himself made this distinction. After His resurrection, He breathed on His disciples and said, *"Receive the Holy Spirit"* (John 20:22 NKJV). At that moment, the Spirit within them brought new life. But then, only days later, He told the same disciples to wait in Jerusalem until they were *"clothed with power from on high"* (Luke 24:49 NIV).

Why wait if they had already received the Spirit? Because the Spirit within is for transformation, but the Spirit upon is for demonstration. The Spirit within makes you holy; the Spirit upon makes you bold. The Spirit within forms Christ in you; the Spirit upon reveals Christ through you.

The Promise of Power

Acts 1:8 is the clearest statement Jesus gave about the Spirit upon:

"But you will receive power when the Holy Spirit has come upon you; and you shall be My witnesses both in Jerusalem, and in all Judea and Samaria, and even to the remotest part of the earth."

Notice the order: power upon, then witness. Jesus didn't tell His disciples to go out and try their best. He didn't send them on mission armed only with memories of His teaching. He told them to wait for power.

Power here is dunamis in Greek—the word from which we get dynamite. Explosive, supernatural, divine energy. This isn't human charisma or natural skill. This is heaven's power resting on human vessels.

The Spirit upon equips you to be a witness—not just in words, but in demonstration. Witnesses don't argue a case they've only read about. They testify to what they've seen and heard. The Spirit upon turns you into a living witness of the risen Christ, demonstrating His kingdom with signs, wonders, and bold proclamation.

Pentecost: The Spirit Falls

Acts 2 records the fulfillment of Jesus' promise. The disciples gathered in an upper room, waiting. Suddenly, a sound like a rushing wind filled the place. Tongues of fire appeared and rested upon each one. They were all filled with the Holy Spirit and began to speak in other tongues as the Spirit gave utterance.

This moment was more than emotional ecstasy. It was the

birth of the Church in power. Immediately, Peter—once timid and fearful—stood and preached boldly. Three thousand were saved in a single day. The Spirit upon turned a group of hiding disciples into a movement that shook empires.

The pattern is clear: Spirit within gives life; Spirit upon gives power. The Spirit within makes you a child of God; the Spirit upon makes you an ambassador of His kingdom.

The Anointing for Assignment

Throughout Scripture, when the Spirit came upon someone, it was for a task, an assignment, a demonstration.

- The Spirit came upon Gideon, and he led Israel into battle.
- The Spirit came upon Samson, and he tore lions apart with his bare hands.
- The Spirit came upon David, and he ruled as king and wrote psalms that carried heaven's heart.
- The Spirit came upon prophets, and they spoke words that shifted nations.

Now, in Christ, the Spirit does not just come upon a select few for select moments. He comes upon all believers, equipping us for the assignment of bearing witness to Jesus.

The anointing is not for entertainment. It is not for status. It is not a badge of spirituality. It is empowerment for mission. The Spirit upon you is heaven's endorsement to represent the King and His kingdom in your generation.

Boldness: The First Evidence

In Acts 4, after Peter and John were threatened by religious leaders, the believers gathered to pray. They asked God for boldness. The place shook, they were filled with the Holy Spirit again, and they spoke the word of God with boldness.

Notice: they didn't pray for safety. They didn't pray for comfort. They prayed for boldness. And the Spirit came upon them again to grant it.

Boldness is the first evidence of the Spirit upon your life. You stop living timidly. You stop hiding your faith. You stop watering down the gospel. You find yourself declaring Jesus with clarity and courage, even in the face of opposition.

This doesn't mean you become brash or careless. Boldness is not arrogance. It is Spirit-empowered courage rooted in love. It is the willingness to speak truth even when it costs.

Gifts for Demonstration

The Spirit upon also manifests in gifts that demonstrate the kingdom. Paul lists them in 1 Corinthians 12: word of wisdom, word of knowledge, faith, healing, miracles, prophecy, discerning of spirits, tongues, and interpretation of tongues.

These gifts are not medals of honor. They are tools of service. They are not about proving your spirituality. They are about serving people with heaven's resources.

When you move in a word of knowledge, you unlock a person's heart to the reality that God sees them. When you pray for healing and the sick recover, you demonstrate that the kingdom of God is near. When you prophesy, you strengthen and encourage. Each gift is a key that unlocks heaven on earth.

This is why Jesus said, *"Heal the sick, raise the dead, cleanse the lepers, cast out demons. Freely you have received; freely give."* *(Matthew 10:8 NKJV).* The Spirit upon is for giving away what you have received.

In and Upon: Working Together

It's important to see how the Spirit within and the Spirit upon work together. They are not in competition; they are in harmony.

The Spirit within shapes your character; the Spirit upon releases your calling. The Spirit within forms fruit; the Spirit upon empowers gifts. The Spirit within makes you holy; the Spirit upon makes you bold.

If you emphasize the Spirit upon without the Spirit within, you may burn bright but burn out—or worse, burn others. If you emphasize the Spirit within without the Spirit upon, you may grow holy but remain ineffective in mission. God's design is both: formation and demonstration, intimacy and power, holiness and boldness.

Receiving the Spirit Upon

So how do we receive the Spirit upon? The book of Acts gives us several keys:

1. Wait in Hunger. The disciples were told to wait in Jerusalem until the Spirit came. Hunger creates space for His power.
2. Ask. Jesus said in Luke 11:13, *"How much more will your Father in heaven give the Holy Spirit to those who ask him!"* Ask boldly.

3. Yield. The Spirit comes upon yielded vessels. Surrender your agenda, your pride, your control.
4. Believe. Receive by faith. The Spirit is a gift, not a wage. You don't earn Him—you receive Him.
5. Be Filled Again. Acts shows multiple fillings. Don't rely on yesterday's encounter. Keep asking, keep receiving.

The baptism of the Spirit is both an event and a lifestyle. You may have a dramatic moment of encounter, but you also need continual infillings. Just as your body needs fresh bread daily, your spirit needs fresh empowerment daily.

Walking in Power and Purpose

Once the Spirit comes upon you, you must steward His presence. Power without purpose is wasted. Boldness without love is harmful. Gifts without fruit are empty.

How do you walk in power and purpose?

- Stay Rooted in Intimacy. Never let the Spirit upon distract you from the Spirit within. Power must flow from presence.
- Keep the Mission Central. The Spirit upon is for witness. Don't make it about your brand. Make it about His name.
- Use the Keys. Remember: the Spirit upon gives you keys of authority. Use them to bind and loose, to release heaven's ways into earth's situations.
- Stay Dependent. Power is not a possession; it is a partnership. Stay reliant on the Spirit daily.

Modern Pentecosts

History is filled with examples of believers who experienced the Spirit upon and changed the world.

- On New Year's Eve, 1900, students at Bethel Bible School in Topeka, Kansas, prayed for the baptism of the Spirit. Agnes Ozman began speaking in tongues, and a Pentecostal wave spread across the globe.
- In 1906, a small gathering at Azusa Street in Los Angeles exploded into a revival marked by healings, tongues, and racial reconciliation. From there, Pentecostal fire spread to every continent.
- Today, millions upon millions testify to encounters with the Spirit upon that launched them into bold witness and supernatural ministry.

The same Spirit is available to you. The same fire that fell in Acts 2 and Azusa Street can rest upon your life.

Reflection Questions

1. How do you understand the difference between the Spirit within and the Spirit upon?
2. Why do you think Jesus told His disciples to wait for power before witnessing?
3. Have you experienced the Spirit upon your life? What changed afterward?
4. Which gifts of the Spirit have you seen in operation through your life? Which do you hunger for more of?
5. How can you steward the Spirit's power with humility and purpose?

Prayer

Holy Spirit, I thank You for living within me, forming Christ in me. But I also ask for You to come upon me in power. Baptize me afresh in Your fire. Clothe me with boldness to be a witness. Release Your gifts through me to heal, to prophesy, to deliver, to encourage. Let my life demonstrate the kingdom of God, not in word only, but in power. Keep me rooted in intimacy, grounded in holiness, and bold in mission. In Jesus' name, amen.

Declarations

- The Spirit is within me for transformation and upon me for demonstration.
- I am clothed with power from on high to be a witness of Jesus.
- Boldness is my portion; fear will not silence me.
- The gifts of the Spirit flow through me to serve and build others.
- I steward the Spirit's power with humility, intimacy, and love.
- I walk in the authority of the kingdom, releasing heaven on earth.

CHAPTER 6
GRIEVE OR QUENCH? GUARDING THE FLOW

When you came to Christ, the Spirit of God took up residence within you. When you were baptized in His power, the Spirit came upon you to make you a witness. This means every believer is called to live in a continual flow of the Spirit—life within, power upon.

But if we are honest, many believers experience interruptions in that flow. They go through seasons where God feels distant, their prayers seem dry, or the power of the Spirit seems absent. Sometimes this leads them to question: "Did I lose the Spirit? Has God abandoned me?"

The good news is this: if you are in Christ, His Spirit has not abandoned you. The Spirit within is God's seal of your salvation (Ephesians 1:13). He doesn't leave when you fail. But the New Testament warns that you can grieve Him (Ephesians 4:30) and quench Him (1 Thessalonians 5:19 NIV). Both of these hinder His flow in your life and through your life.

Guarding the flow of the Spirit is essential for walking in the purpose and power of the believer.

What It Means to Grieve the Spirit

Ephesians 4:30* says: *"Do not grieve the Holy Spirit of God, with whom you were sealed for the day of redemption."*

To grieve is to cause sorrow, to bring pain to the heart. The Spirit is not an impersonal force; He is a Person. He feels. He loves. He desires fellowship with you. And like any close relationship, He can be grieved when you choose what is contrary to His nature.

Paul mentions this in the context of putting off the old life: bitterness, anger, slander, sexual immorality, dishonesty. When we engage in sin, we are living against the Spirit who lives within us. He doesn't abandon us, but He is grieved.

Think of it like a marriage. When a spouse acts in betrayal, the covenant remains, but intimacy is wounded. Trust is broken. Joy is disrupted. The relationship suffers. In the same way, sin grieves the Spirit and disrupts the intimacy He longs to share with you.

Grieving the Spirit primarily affects the inward flow—your intimacy, sensitivity, and fellowship with Him.

What It Means to Quench the Spirit

1 Thessalonians 5:19† gives a simple but sobering command: *"Do not quench the Spirit."*

The word "quench" means to extinguish, like putting out a

---

*   NIV
†   NKJV

fire. The Spirit is often pictured as fire, and Paul warns believers not to put that fire out.

We quench the Spirit when we resist His movements. When He prompts us to speak and we stay silent. When He nudges us to pray for someone and we walk away. When He stirs us to step out in faith and we hold back in fear.

Quenching is not about sin in general—that grieves Him. Quenching is specifically about resistance to His outward activity. It is saying "no" when He is trying to move through you.

Think about Acts 4. The believers prayed for boldness, and the Spirit came upon them, filling them with courage. What if they had resisted? What if they had chosen silence out of fear? That would have quenched the Spirit's fire.

Quenching the Spirit primarily affects the outward flow—the demonstration of power, boldness, and gifts through your life.

Grieve and Quench: How They Work Together

Though grieving and quenching are distinct, they are often connected. A heart grieved by hidden sin often becomes a heart that quenches outward expression. Why? Because compromise on the inside breeds resistance on the outside.

If you've been living with unconfessed sin, shame often silences boldness. If you've been ignoring the Spirit's whispers, it becomes easier to ignore His nudges. Grieving leads to quenching.

Conversely, quenching can lead to grieving. If you consistently resist His movements outwardly, your heart can grow dull inwardly. Sensitivity fades. Hunger diminishes. Over time, you can find yourself going through the motions of faith but without fire.

This is why Paul addresses both. Guarding the flow means tending to both inward holiness and outward obedience.

Three Major Blockages: Compromise, Distraction, and Fear

1. Compromise

Compromise is living with one foot in the kingdom and one foot in the world. It is tolerating sin that you know the Spirit has called you to leave behind. Compromise grieves Him because it makes room for darkness in the temple of God.

It may not even be "big" sins—often it's subtle things: cutting corners at work, feeding lust through media, harboring bitterness, nursing offense. These are leaks in your intimacy with the Spirit.

2. Distraction

Even without gross sin, distraction can dull your sensitivity. A heart constantly occupied with noise, screens, busyness, and worry has little space to notice the Spirit's voice. Jesus warned that the cares of life can choke the word and make it unfruitful (Mark 4:19).

The Spirit is gentle. He does not shout over the chaos. He waits for attention. A distracted heart quenches His flame simply by ignoring it.

3. Fear

Fear quenches the Spirit more than almost anything else. Fear of man—what will they think if I step out? Fear of failure —what if nothing happens when I pray? Fear of deception— what if I get it wrong?

Fear is agreement with lies. It keeps believers passive when the Spirit is urging them to act. Fear quenches boldness and silences testimony.

Guarding the Flow

How do we guard the flow of the Spirit? The answer is not striving harder but cultivating rhythms of repentance, attentiveness, and obedience.

1. Quick Repentance. Keep short accounts with God. When the Spirit convicts, don't delay. Confess, turn, and receive forgiveness. Don't let sin fester.
2. Daily Attention. Give space to listen. Silence the noise. Create moments where the Spirit has your full focus.
3. Obedience in the Small. The best way to guard the outward flow is to say "yes" in little nudges. Obey quickly. Obedience builds sensitivity.
4. Community Accountability. Isolation breeds compromise. Accountability with trusted brothers and sisters keeps your heart clear and your obedience sharp.

A Repentance Liturgy

Here's a simple liturgy you can pray regularly:

- Father, I acknowledge where I have grieved Your Spirit. (Pause. Let Him bring things to mind. Confess them honestly.)
- I receive the cleansing of Jesus' blood. (Thank Him for forgiveness. Picture Him washing you clean.)
- Holy Spirit, sensitize my heart again. (Ask Him to restore tenderness and awareness.)
- I renounce every lie and agreement with fear. (Break agreement with fear, pride, or unbelief.)
- I choose obedience today. (Declare your yes to His voice, even in the small things.)

Praying this regularly keeps your heart clear, your intimacy fresh, and your courage sharp.

Accountability Rhythms

Repentance is personal, but accountability is relational. God designed you to walk with others who help guard the flow. Here are some rhythms to cultivate:

- Confession Partners. Have one or two trusted believers you can confess sin to, as James 5:16 says: *"Confess your sins to each other and pray for each other so that you may be healed."*
- Obedience Check-Ins. Share what the Spirit is asking of you, and let others ask if you followed through.
- Corporate Listening. Gather in groups to ask, *"Holy Spirit, what are You saying to us?"* Shared discernment reduces error and increases courage.

Accountability is not legalism; it is family. It's how we guard each other from deception, dullness, and drift.

Reflection Questions

1. What does it mean to you personally to grieve the Spirit? Can you recall a time when you felt the weight of that grief?
2. Have you ever quenched the Spirit by resisting His nudge? What happened afterward?
3. Which of the three blockages—compromise, distraction, or fear—tends to challenge you most?
4. What rhythms of repentance or accountability do you need to establish to guard the flow of the Spirit?
5. How would your life look different if the Spirit's flow was fully unblocked within and upon you?

Prayer

Holy Spirit, I honor You as the One who lives within me and rests upon me. Forgive me for the times I have grieved You with sin or quenched You with resistance. Wash me clean by the blood of Jesus. Sensitize my heart again. Ignite Your fire afresh in me. Give me courage to obey quickly, tenderness to repent deeply, and wisdom to walk in community. Let nothing block the flow of Your presence and power through my life. In Jesus' name, amen.

Declarations

- I will not grieve the Spirit; I choose holiness and purity.
- I will not quench the Spirit; I choose bold obedience.
- My heart is tender, my ears are open, my will is surrendered.
- Compromise, distraction, and fear have no hold on me.
- The Spirit's flow within me and upon me is unblocked and free.
- I live as a vessel of intimacy and a channel of power.

PART THREE
HOSTING THE PRESENCE: A LIFESTYLE THAT BRINGS HEAVEN NEAR

CHAPTER 7
THE GREENHOUSE HOME

When you think of revival, you might picture stadiums full of worshipers, crusades in city squares, or churches packed with hungry people. And while those moments matter, the presence of God was never meant to be confined to a service or an event. His presence was meant to saturate your daily life—including the very atmosphere of your home.

Your home can become what I call a greenhouse of the kingdom. A greenhouse is an environment where conditions are intentionally cultivated so life that could not survive outside can thrive inside. It shields fragile plants from harsh weather, concentrates warmth and light, and creates space for growth that would otherwise be impossible.

The same can be true of your home. In a world filled with spiritual coldness, fear, compromise, and distraction, your home can be a greenhouse of God's presence. A place where His peace reigns. A place where healing happens. A place where even unbelievers who walk in can sense, "Something is different here."

This is not reserved for pastors or prophets. It is God's intent for every believer. Any home can host the presence of God like Eden once did.

The Home as God's Dwelling

From the beginning, God's desire has been to dwell with His people. Eden was not just a garden—it was God's dwelling place with humanity. Heaven and earth overlapped, and Adam and Eve walked with Him without separation.

After the fall, that overlap was broken. Yet God's desire never changed. He tabernacled with Israel in a tent, later in the temple. Then, in Jesus, "*the Word became flesh and dwelt (literally, tabernacled) among us*" (John 1:14 NIV). And now, by His Spirit, we are the temple. God's presence is not confined to a tent or a temple but fills His people and their spaces.

This means your house is not just a building. It is potential tabernacle space—a place where heaven and earth overlap again.

Consecration: Setting Your Home Apart

The first step to creating a greenhouse home is consecration —setting your home apart for God. Consecration means saying, "This house belongs to You, Lord. It is not just my dwelling—it is Your dwelling."

In the Old Testament, priests consecrated the temple with prayer, sacrifice, and anointing oil. In the New Testament, we consecrate our homes through prayer, worship, and the blood of Jesus.

You can do this by walking through each room and declaring, "This space is set apart for God. Nothing unclean, dark, or demonic has a right to dwell here. Only the Spirit of God is welcome."

Pray over doorways. Anoint them with oil if you like. Invite the presence of God into every corner. Consecration is not about ritual—it is about intentionality. It is about declaring, "*As for me and my house, we will serve the Lord.*" *(Joshua 24:15 NKJV)*

Cleansing: Removing What Doesn't Belong

Consecration is powerful, but it must be paired with cleansing. A greenhouse must be kept free from pests, mold, and decay, or the plants inside will wither. Likewise, your home must be cleansed of what does not belong to the kingdom.

This means physically and spiritually removing items, influences, or atmospheres that grieve or quench the Spirit.

Ask the Spirit: "Is there anything in this home that does not belong?" He may highlight certain media, books, objects tied to occult or idolatry, or simply things that stir compromise. He may point to habits—constant TV noise, toxic arguments, or words spoken in anger—that create atmospheres hostile to His presence.

Don't get superstitious, but don't ignore conviction. If He says something needs to go, remove it. Sometimes the greatest breakthroughs come not from adding more but from removing what hinders.

Think of Jesus cleansing the temple. He overturned tables, drove out what corrupted, and declared, "My Father's house shall be called a house of prayer." Your home can carry the same reality.

Blessing: Filling with His Presence

Once a home is consecrated and cleansed, it must be filled. Jesus warned that if a house swept clean is left empty, it may be re-inhabited by worse influences (Matthew 12:44–45). The answer is to fill it with God's presence.

How do you bless your home? By filling it with prayer, worship, Scripture, and thanksgiving.

- Play worship music that exalts Jesus.
- Read Scripture aloud in your living spaces.
- Speak blessings over your family, guests, and even objects—your table, your bed, your children's rooms.
- Invite the Spirit daily: "Holy Spirit, You are welcome here."

This isn't superstition; it's atmosphere-setting. Just as a greenhouse requires consistent warmth and light, your home thrives when it is consistently filled with God's presence.

A Practical Walkthrough: Room-by-Room Prayers

Here's a guide you can use to consecrate, cleanse, and bless your home.

Front Door / Entryway
Pray: "Lord, may everyone who enters here encounter Your peace. Let this doorway be a threshold of blessing. No spirit of darkness has permission to cross this threshold."

Living Room

Pray: "Jesus, be the center of our fellowship. May conversations here be full of love, encouragement, and truth. Let this space host joy and laughter that glorifies You."

Kitchen / Dining Area

Pray: "Father, thank You for provision. We invite You to every meal. Let this table be a place of connection, gratitude, and hospitality."

Bedrooms

Pray: "Lord, may this room be filled with rest and safety. Drive out every fear, anxiety, or torment. Let dreams be sanctified and hearts refreshed."

Children's Rooms

Pray: "Jesus, cover these children with Your presence. Let angels stand guard. Let this room be filled with songs of joy and learning of Your ways."

Office / Workspace

Pray: "Lord, establish the work of our hands. Let everything created here be done in integrity and excellence. Let this space release creativity inspired by heaven."

Bathrooms

Pray: "God, thank You for cleansing and refreshing. May even this space remind us that You wash us clean."

Backyard / Outdoor Spaces

Pray: "Lord, let this land be fruitful and protected. May it be a place of rest, play, and reflection of Your beauty."

Atmosphere Shifts

The goal is more than a one-time prayer walk. Hosting the presence is about cultivating atmosphere daily.

- Worship regularly. Play songs that glorify Jesus. Atmosphere shifts when His name is exalted.
- Guard conversations. Refuse gossip, slander, or constant complaining. Words shape the air you breathe.
- Practice gratitude. Thankfulness is a magnet for the Spirit. Keep thanksgiving flowing in your home.
- Pray out loud. Whispered prayers matter, but declarations shift atmospheres. Pray Scripture over your house.
- Rest. A greenhouse must maintain balance. Build rhythms of Sabbath and quiet.

When you guard your atmosphere, your home becomes a refuge—not just for you, but for everyone who enters.

Testimony of a Greenhouse Home

I'll never forget a story one of our church members told me. A delivery man dropped off a package at her house. As he stepped into the entryway, he froze. "What is that I feel? It's so peaceful here," he asked. She smiled and told him, "That's the presence of Jesus." He left different than he came.

This is what it means for your home to become a greenhouse. Even those who don't yet know Christ will encounter Him when they enter your space. Your house becomes a thin place where heaven and earth overlap.

Reflection Questions

1. Does your home currently feel like a greenhouse for God's presence, or more like just a place to eat and sleep?
2. What would it look like to consecrate your home afresh to the Lord?
3. Are there objects, habits, or atmospheres in your home that the Spirit may want to cleanse?
4. Which room in your home most needs the blessing of God's presence right now?
5. How can you establish daily or weekly rhythms that keep the atmosphere of your home filled with worship and prayer?

Prayer

Father, I thank You for the gift of my home. I set it apart for You. Every room, every wall, every piece of furniture belongs to You. Lord Jesus, cleanse this house of anything that does not honor You. Remove every dark influence and fill this place with Your Spirit. May my home be a greenhouse of Your kingdom—a refuge of peace, a sanctuary of worship, a place where heaven touches earth. In Jesus' name, amen.

Declarations

- My home is consecrated to the Lord.
- No spirit of darkness has permission to dwell here.
- The presence of God fills every room of my house.
- My home is a greenhouse of peace, joy, and healing.
- Everyone who enters my home will encounter the love of Jesus.
- As for me and my house, we will serve the Lord.

CHAPTER 8
HOLY HABITS OF A PRESENCE PEOPLE

I f you want your life and your home to be a greenhouse of God's presence, it won't happen by accident. Atmosphere doesn't just appear—it's cultivated. Presence is a gift, but it must also be stewarded. Like a flame on an altar, it needs fuel, protection, and attention.

Jesus told us in John 15: *"Abide in Me, and I in you. As the branch cannot bear fruit of itself unless it abides in the vine, neither can you, unless you abide in Me."** Presence people are abiding people. We don't just visit God on Sundays. We don't just call on Him when we're desperate. We abide—we make Him our dwelling place.

The early Church was not sustained by hype or events. They were sustained by holy habits—daily rhythms that turned their attention toward God, cultivated awareness of His Spirit, and allowed His presence to shape their lives. These habits are not about legalism or earning. They are about align-

---

* NKJV

They keep us close to the Vine so that fruit naturally grows.

Let's explore what it means to abide, adore, and attend—and then we'll get practical about the habits that cultivate a lifestyle of presence.

Abide: Staying Connected

To abide means to remain, to stay connected, to dwell. A branch cannot survive cut off from the vine. In the same way, believers cannot thrive apart from the presence of Jesus.

Abiding is not a moment—it's a posture. It's not just reading your Bible in the morning and then forgetting God all day. It's walking in continual awareness: "He is with me. He is in me. He is upon me."

Abiding means we stop treating God as a visitor and start treating Him as the homeowner. He doesn't just come and go—He lives here. And when you live with that awareness, everything changes.

Adore: Lifting Him Up

Abiding naturally leads to adoration. If you dwell in His presence, you can't help but worship. To adore is to set your affection on Him, to let your heart overflow with love, gratitude, and honor.

Psalm 27:4 says, "One thing I ask from the Lord, this only do I seek: that I may dwell in the house of the Lord all the days of my life, to gaze on the beauty of the Lord and to seek Him in His temple." NIV

Adoration is not just singing songs. It is learning to see His

HOLY HABITS OF A PRESENCE PEOPLE   69

beauty everywhere. It is slowing down long enough to gaze at Him. It is giving Him the highest place in your heart, again and again.

A presence people are an adoring people. We don't just ask God to do things for us—we enjoy Him for who He is.

Attend: Paying Attention

Abiding and adoring prepare us for attending—giving our attention to His voice and His movements. Attention is one of the rarest commodities in our distracted age. Phones, screens, and noise compete for every second. But those who cultivate the presence are those who learn to give God their attention.

Isaiah 30:21* says, *"Your ears shall hear a word behind you, saying, 'This is the way, walk in it,' when you turn to the right or when you turn to the left."* That kind of guidance doesn't come when your heart is perpetually distracted. It comes when you attend—when you stop, listen, and notice.

Presence people are attentive people. We learn to hear His whispers, notice His nudges, and follow His lead quickly.

Holy Habits: The Rule of Life

How do we actually cultivate abiding, adoring, and attending? By adopting holy habits—a "rule of life."

A rule of life is not a list of religious duties. The word "rule" comes from a Latin word meaning "trellis." A trellis doesn't

---

* NKJV

produce fruit, but it creates structure for the vine to grow. Habits are like a trellis that support the life of God in you.

Here are five key habits for a presence people:

1. Scripture. God's Word is the clearest revelation of His heart. Daily time in Scripture renews your mind, anchors your soul, and keeps you aligned with His voice.
2. Silence and Solitude. Quiet spaces allow you to hear His whispers and unclutter your soul. Jesus often withdrew to lonely places to pray.
3. Sabbath. Rest is not optional; it is holy. A weekly rhythm of Sabbath keeps you dependent, refreshed, and centered on God's provision.
4. Sacrament. Regular practices like communion, prayer, and even shared meals remind us of Christ's presence in tangible ways.
5. Service. Presence overflows in love for others. Serving is not a distraction from His presence—it is an expression of it.

Scripture: Feeding on the Word

Jesus said, *"Man shall not live by bread alone, but by every word that proceeds from the mouth of God." (Matthew 4:4 NKJV).* Scripture is not just information—it is nourishment.

Make it a daily rhythm. Whether you read a chapter, meditate on a verse, or listen to the Bible while you drive, let the Word shape you. Approach it not as a box to check, but as a conversation with the Author. Ask: "Holy Spirit, what are You saying to me today?"

Presence people feed on the Word until it becomes part of them.

Silence and Solitude: Clearing Space

Noise drowns out the voice of God. That's why silence and solitude are holy habits. When you unplug from the constant buzz, you make room for the Spirit's whisper.

This doesn't mean you need hours of monk-like silence every day. Start with five minutes in the morning. Sit quietly. Breathe deeply. Say, "Here I am, Lord." Over time, lengthen those moments.

In stillness, you'll find that His presence becomes more tangible. Your heart will become more sensitive. And you'll discover that silence is not emptiness—it's space for Him to speak.

Sabbath: Resting in God

Sabbath is one of the most countercultural habits you can adopt. In a world that glorifies busyness, Sabbath declares, "My worth is not in my work—it's in God."

One day each week, cease striving. Don't just stop working; stop worrying. Make space for worship, rest, family, and joy. Sabbath is not laziness—it's trust. It's saying, "God can run the world without me for 24 hours."

Sabbath re-centers your heart, restores your soul, and renews your awareness of His presence.

Sacrament: Tangible Grace

The early Church "devoted themselves to the apostles' teaching and to fellowship, to the breaking of bread and to prayer" (Acts 2:42). They lived sacramentally—experiencing God through physical acts.

Take communion at home. Share meals with thanksgiving. Light a candle as a reminder of His presence. Kneel in prayer. These embodied practices remind us that God is not just an idea—He is present.

Sacramental habits anchor spiritual reality in physical experience. They train your whole self—body, soul, and spirit —to live in His presence.

Service: Presence Overflowing

Finally, presence must overflow in service. Jesus washed His disciples' feet and told them to do likewise. Presence people don't just soak; they serve.

Serving others—whether through acts of kindness, hospitality, or generosity—is a holy habit that keeps your heart soft and aligned with God's love. When you serve, you become His hands and feet. And often, His presence becomes tangible in those very moments.

Building Your Rule of Life

Don't try to adopt every habit at once. Start simple. Pick one or two rhythms you can practice consistently. Over time, build your own "rule of life"—a trellis of habits that keep you abiding, adoring, and attending.

Ask yourself:

- What habits help me notice God's presence?
- What habits stir my affection for Jesus?
- What habits protect my heart from distraction?

Write them down. Share them with a friend. Review them regularly. Your rule of life is not a prison—it's a pathway. It creates space for the Spirit to flow.

Reflection Questions

1. Which of the three postures—abide, adore, attend—do you find easiest? Which is hardest?
2. Which of the five habits (Scripture, silence, Sabbath, sacrament, service) most needs strengthening in your life right now?
3. How could you practically begin a simple "rule of life" this week?
4. What would change in your awareness of God if you added even 10 minutes of silence daily?
5. How can your habits not only shape your private life but also the atmosphere of your home?

Prayer

Lord, I want to be a person of Your presence. Teach me to abide in You daily, to adore You with all my heart, and to attend to Your voice with sensitivity. Show me which habits will help me cultivate a life that honors You and makes space for Your Spirit. Give me grace to practice them with joy, not legalism. Form in me a trellis on which the fruit of Your Spirit can grow strong and lasting. In Jesus' name, amen.

Declarations

- I am a branch connected to the Vine; His life flows through me.
- My heart is set to abide, adore, and attend.
- Scripture feeds me, silence centers me, Sabbath restores me, sacrament grounds me, and service overflows from me.
- My habits are not a burden—they are a trellis for God's life to grow.
- My home and my life are filled with rhythms that cultivate His presence.

CHAPTER 9
HEARING & OBEYING: THE MICRO-YES THAT MOVES MOUNTAINS

One of the greatest privileges of being a child of God is that you can hear His voice. Jesus declared in John 10:27: *"My sheep hear My voice, and I know them, and they follow Me."* Notice how Jesus doesn't say, "Some of My sheep hear My voice" or "the really spiritual sheep hear My voice." He says simply, "My sheep hear My voice." If you belong to Jesus, you have the capacity to hear Him.

But hearing is only the first step. The life of the kingdom hinges not just on hearing but on obeying. The power is in the yes. And not just in the big yes of surrendering your life to Christ, but in the countless small yeses—what I call the micro-yes.

The kingdom advances one micro-yes at a time. A nudge to pray for a coworker. A whisper to give a word of encouragement. A conviction to forgive when you'd rather stay offended. These may seem small, but they are the hinges on which God swings open great doors.

---

* NKJV

Most breakthroughs don't start with a dramatic vision or a booming voice from heaven. They start with a simple nudge, a micro-yes. And when you learn to hear and obey quickly, you become a vessel for heaven's invasion in the earth.

The God Who Speaks

From Genesis to Revelation, we see a God who speaks. He spoke creation into existence. He walked with Adam and Eve in the cool of the day. He called Abraham by name. He gave Moses detailed instructions on the mountain. He spoke through prophets, dreams, visions, and angelic visitations.

And in these last days, He has spoken to us through His Son (Hebrews 1:2). Jesus is the Word made flesh. And after His resurrection, He poured out His Spirit so that His sheep would continue to hear His voice.

The Spirit did not stop speaking when the last apostle died. The Spirit is the One Jesus promised would guide us into all truth, remind us of His words, and reveal what is to come (John 16:13). God is still speaking. The question is: are we listening?

The Simplicity of His Voice

Many believers miss God's voice because they expect it to be complicated. They think hearing God is only for prophets or pastors. Or they wait for a booming voice or dramatic sign. But most often, God's voice comes as a gentle whisper, a nudge, a thought impressed by the Spirit.

Elijah discovered this in 1 Kings 19. God was not in the wind, earthquake, or fire—but in the still small voice.

His voice is often simple:

- "Pray for that person."
- "Call your mom."
- "Don't watch that show."
- "Read this scripture."
- "Give that money."

The simplicity is part of the beauty. He is not trying to confuse you. He is guiding you like a shepherd guides his sheep —clear enough for you to follow if you are willing to listen.

Why Obedience Matters

James 1:22 warns: *"Do not merely listen to the word, and so deceive yourselves. Do what it says."** Hearing without obeying is self-deception. It convinces you that proximity to God's word equals transformation, when in reality transformation comes through obedience.

Obedience is the hinge of kingdom life. It is the point at which heaven meets earth. When you obey, you align your will with God's will, and His kingdom flows through you.

Think about Jesus' first miracle. At Cana, He turned water into wine. But the miracle hinged on Mary's words to the servants: *"Do whatever He tells you."* Their obedience to a seemingly strange instruction—fill jars with water—opened the door for glory to be revealed.

That's the pattern. Heaven breaks in where obedience opens the door.

---

* NIV

The Micro-Yes

Big yeses matter—saying yes to salvation, yes to baptism, yes to your calling. But often, it is the small, daily yeses that shape your life and release heaven.

The Spirit nudges you to forgive when you'd rather stay angry. That micro-yes breaks the chain of bitterness.

He whispers to give $20 to a stranger. That micro-yes opens the floodgate of provision.

He prompts you to share your testimony with a coworker. That micro-yes could alter eternity for them.

The micro-yes is powerful because it builds momentum. Each time you say yes, you become more sensitive, more courageous, more aligned. Over time, micro-yeses accumulate into a lifestyle of radical obedience.

Delayed Obedience Is Disobedience

One of the greatest ways we quench the Spirit is by delaying obedience. We feel the nudge, but we wait. We rationalize. We say, "I'll do it later." But later often never comes.

Delayed obedience is really disobedience in disguise. The Spirit's timing is intentional. If He prompts you to act now, it's because someone needs heaven's touch now.

That's why I encourage the practice of 90-second obedience. When you sense the Spirit prompting you, act within 90 seconds. Send the text. Say the prayer. Step out in faith. The longer you wait, the more likely fear, doubt, or distraction will talk you out of it.

Testing and Discerning

Of course, we must test what we hear. Not every thought is from God. Scripture is our anchor. The Spirit never contradicts the Word. Wise counsel helps confirm. Inner peace often signals alignment.

But don't use testing as an excuse for inaction. Many believers hide passivity behind endless "discerning." At some point, you must step out. Faith is spelled R-I-S-K.

If you get it wrong, God is gracious. He is a Father training His children. He doesn't shame you for trying to obey. He delights in your yes, even when it's imperfect.

Stories of Obedience

I've seen time and again how micro-yeses release heaven. I remember once feeling a nudge to stop and pray for a man at a gas station. It was inconvenient. I was tired. But I obeyed. As I prayed, tears filled his eyes. He confessed he had been asking God for a sign that He still cared. That moment shifted his life.

Another time, I felt the Spirit whisper during service: "Call the young man to the front. Lay hands on him." I obeyed. The Spirit came upon him powerfully, breaking chains of addiction. That one yes led to a ripple of transformation in his family.

These are not about me—they are about what God does through simple obedience. And they are available to you.

Building a Lifestyle of Obedience

Hearing and obeying is not about occasional moments—it's about cultivating a lifestyle. Here are some practices to help:

1. Start your day with surrender. Before the noise begins, pray: "Lord, my answer today is yes. Whatever You ask, I will obey."
2. Listen throughout the day. Ask, "Holy Spirit, what are You saying right now?" Pay attention to thoughts, impressions, and nudges.
3. Act quickly. Practice 90-second obedience. Don't overthink. Trust and act.
4. Journal your yeses. Write down the moments you obeyed, what happened, and what you learned. This builds faith and testimony.
5. Share with others. Obedience grows in community. Share your yeses and celebrate together.

Obedience and Authority

There is a direct connection between obedience and spiritual authority. Acts 5:32 says, *"We are witnesses of these things, and so is the Holy Spirit, whom God has given to those who obey Him." NKJV*

The Spirit rests on obedient vessels. Authority is not about titles or positions—it is about surrendered lives. When you consistently say yes, the Spirit entrusts you with greater assignments.

Reflection Questions

1. When was the last time you sensed God speaking to you? How did you respond?
2. What excuses or fears most often keep you from immediate obedience?
3. How might your life look different if you practiced 90-second obedience this week?
4. What small yes is the Spirit prompting you to give today?
5. Who could you invite into your obedience journey for encouragement and accountability?

Prayer

Jesus, thank You that You are my Shepherd and I am Your sheep. Thank You that I can hear Your voice. Forgive me for the times I have delayed or resisted obedience. Teach me to live with a tender ear and a quick yes. Holy Spirit, sensitize me to Your whispers and give me courage to obey within seconds. Let my micro-yeses release heaven's reality in my life and in the lives of those around me. In Jesus' name, amen.

Declarations

- I am a sheep who hears the Shepherd's voice.
- I will obey quickly and joyfully.
- My micro-yeses open the door for heaven to invade earth.
- Fear, doubt, and delay will not silence my obedience.
- The Spirit is training me to walk in step with Him daily.
- Every yes I give builds momentum for breakthrough.

CHAPTER 10
CLEAN HANDS, PURE HEART: RIGHTEOUSNESS THAT HOSTS POWER

There's a question that echoes across the Scriptures, one that strikes at the very core of what it means to live as a presence-filled believer: *"Who may ascend the hill of the Lord? Who may stand in His holy place?"* (Psalm 24:3 NIV).

The answer is equally striking: *"He who has clean hands and a pure heart, who does not lift up his soul to what is false and does not swear deceitfully. He will receive blessing from the Lord and righteousness from the God of his salvation."* (Psalm 24:4–5 ESV).

This is not just poetic imagery. It is a Kingdom reality. The presence of God rests on people who live with integrity. The Spirit moves in power through vessels that are consecrated. Clean hands and pure hearts are not optional extras for the "super-spiritual"—they are the foundation for carrying the authority of the Kingdom.

God delights to pour His Spirit upon His sons and daughters, but He will not empower what He cannot endorse. Compromise grieves Him. Hypocrisy quenches Him. Sin separates—not because He doesn't love us, but because His nature is holy. To host His presence and steward His power, we must walk in holiness and integrity.

Why Righteousness Matters

Throughout Scripture, there is a consistent pattern: God entrusts authority to those who walk uprightly before Him.

- Joseph resisted compromise in Potiphar's house. He endured false accusation and prison, but his integrity positioned him to carry authority over Egypt.
- Daniel refused to defile himself with the king's food. His holiness opened the way for him to stand before kings and release prophetic wisdom.
- Jesus Himself was tempted in every way, yet without sin. Because He walked in purity, the Spirit rested upon Him without measure (John 3:34).

Authority flows through clean vessels. Compromise may not keep you from being loved by God, but it will keep you from being trusted with Kingdom power.

We live in an age where charisma often outpaces character. Gifts may open doors, but only integrity keeps them open. Anointing may break yokes, but only holiness sustains revival. If we want to host the power of God, we must live lives that reflect the holiness of God.

What Does It Mean to Have Clean Hands?

Clean hands speak of outward integrity. It is about our actions, our choices, and the way we treat others. To have clean hands means:

- We deal honestly in our finances.
- We treat people with respect and love, not manipulation or control.
- We walk in purity with our eyes and our bodies.
- We refuse to use our hands for violence, dishonesty, or selfish gain.

In Scripture, hands represent action. When our actions are righteous, our hands are clean. This doesn't mean perfection—but it does mean integrity. It means living in such a way that there is nothing hidden, nothing we need to cover up. Presence people must guard their actions. Not out of fear of punishment, but out of reverence for the One who rests upon them.

What Does It Mean to Have a Pure Heart?

A pure heart is about inward integrity. While clean hands focus on our actions, a pure heart focuses on our motives. Why do we do what we do?

Jesus said in *Matthew 5:8 ESV: "Blessed are the pure in heart, for they shall see God."* Purity of heart allows us to perceive and host the presence of God.

A pure heart means:

- Our motives are not mixed with selfish ambition.
- We seek God Himself, not just His blessings.
- We desire to please Him above impressing people.
- We quickly repent when we recognize wrong motives.

Purity is about alignment of the inner life. It's possible to have clean hands but not a pure heart—to do the right thing outwardly but for the wrong reasons. God desires both.

Closing Open Doors of Compromise

One of the ways the enemy gains influence in believers' lives is through compromise. Sin opens doors for oppression. Compromise creates cracks in our walls where the enemy can creep in.

Compromise looks like:

- Allowing unforgiveness to linger.
- Entertaining secret sin while trying to look spiritual.
- Justifying what God has clearly called sin.
- Blending the values of the world with the values of the Kingdom.

When we compromise, we grieve the Spirit within us and quench the Spirit upon us. The flow of His presence and power slows. It's not that He leaves us—but His activity in and through us becomes restricted.

To walk in power, we must close the open doors. That means repentance, renunciation, and restoration.

- Repentance: turning from sin and aligning with God's ways.
- Renunciation: verbally breaking agreement with lies or sinful patterns.
- Restoration: making things right where possible— apologizing, reconciling, repaying.

When the doors are closed, the atmosphere clears. The greenhouse of your life becomes pure again. And the Spirit delights to rest on such a dwelling.

Holiness Sustains Power

We live in a culture obsessed with power—political power, financial power, even supernatural power. But God is more concerned with purity than power. Power without holiness corrupts. Holiness without power becomes religious. The Kingdom requires both.

Holiness sustains power because it keeps the vessel aligned with the nature of the Spirit. The Spirit is called the Holy Spirit for a reason. He is holy, and He desires to rest on holy vessels.

This is why revival history is littered with stories of men and women who moved in great power but fell into sin. Their gifting was real. The Spirit moved. But the lack of clean hands and pure hearts eroded the foundation. Eventually, the vessel collapsed under the weight of the anointing.

If we want to walk in lasting power, we must pursue lasting holiness. Not perfection, but consecration. Not striving, but surrender. Not legalism, but love.

Practical Ways to Pursue Holiness and Integrity

Holiness is not about white-knuckled rule-keeping. It is about cultivating a life where His Spirit has full reign. Here are some practical ways to keep your hands clean and your heart pure:

1. Daily Confession and Communion. Take time each day to confess sins and receive the cleansing of Christ's blood. Communion is not just a ritual—it is a renewal of covenant and consecration.
2. Guard Your Eyes and Ears. What you watch, listen to, and meditate on shapes your heart. If it grieves the Spirit, don't consume it.

3. Walk in Transparency. Live in such a way that nothing needs to be hidden. Invite trusted friends or leaders to ask you hard questions.
4. Keep Short Accounts. Don't let unforgiveness linger. Reconcile quickly. Apologize quickly. Forgive quickly.
5. Honor God in Finances. Integrity in money is a major test of the heart. Tithing, generosity, and honesty matter deeply to the Lord.
6. Rest in His Grace. Holiness is not about earning His love. It is about responding to His love. Rest in His finished work as you pursue purity.

Hosting the Presence

Clean hands and pure hearts are not just about morality. They are about hosting the presence of God. When your life is pure, your spirit becomes more sensitive. You notice His whispers. You sense His nudges. You feel His delight.

Purity creates capacity. Integrity sustains influence. Holiness keeps the flow of His Spirit unhindered. And the result is that your life becomes a greenhouse for His presence—a place where heaven is tangible, where others encounter God through you.

Psalm 24 ends with a vision of the King of glory entering in: *"Lift up your heads, you gates; be lifted up, you ancient doors, that the King of glory may come in."** When we close the doors of compromise and lift up the gates of our lives, the King of glory comes in with power.

---

* NIV

Reflection Questions

1. In what areas of your life are your "hands" clean? Where might they need cleansing?
2. Are there hidden motives in your heart that the Spirit is putting His finger on?
3. What compromises have you justified that may be grieving or quenching the Spirit?
4. Which of the practical steps toward holiness do you need to begin this week?
5. How would your awareness of God's presence change if you lived with clean hands and a pure heart daily?

Prayer

Father, I desire to ascend Your holy hill. I want to stand in Your presence without shame. Cleanse my hands, purify my heart, and align my motives with Yours. Expose every compromise and give me the courage to repent, renounce, and restore. Make me a vessel that honors You and hosts Your presence well. Let holiness sustain the power You entrust to me. In Jesus' name, amen.

Declarations

- My hands are clean, and my heart is pure by the blood of Jesus.
- I walk in holiness, not by striving, but by the Spirit.
- Compromise has no place in my life; I close every open door to sin.
- Purity creates capacity in me for God's presence.
- Integrity sustains the authority God entrusts to me.
- I am a dwelling place for the King of glory.

PART FOUR
DEMONSTRATION: SIGNS, WONDERS, AND DISCIPLE-MAKING

CHAPTER 11
THE KING'S WORKS: HEALING THE SICK

When Jesus sent His disciples out, He didn't just tell them to preach the Kingdom—He told them to demonstrate it. *"As you go, proclaim this message: 'The kingdom of heaven has come near.' Heal the sick, raise the dead, cleanse those who have leprosy, drive out demons. Freely you have received; freely give." (Matthew 10:7–8 NIV).*

Healing is not an optional side ministry. It is central to the mission of the Kingdom. Wherever Jesus went, He preached the good news of the Kingdom and healed the sick (Matthew 4:23). The two went hand-in-hand. Healing was not a gimmick to draw crowds—it was the tangible sign that heaven had invaded earth.

In Mark 16:17–18, Jesus promised that signs would accompany those who believe: *"In my name they will lay their hands on the sick, and they will recover."** Healing is the King's work, and He has given His people authority to continue it.

---

* NKJV

Yet many believers hesitate. Some fear they'll pray and nothing will happen. Others think healing is for special "anointed" people. Still others have seen abuses and don't want to be associated with hype. But the truth is simple: healing is the normal outflow of the Kingdom. It is the children's bread (Matthew 15:26). And when we step out in faith, we partner with the Spirit to release the life of heaven into broken bodies.

Healing as a Sign of the Kingdom's Nearness

Healing is not the full Kingdom, but it is a sign of the Kingdom's nearness. Every time someone is healed, it is a preview of the age to come—a glimpse of the New Eden where there will be no more pain, sickness, or tears.

In Revelation 21:4, we see the promise: *"He will wipe every tear from their eyes. There will be no more death or mourning or crying or pain, for the old order of things has passed away."** Healing now points to that day. It doesn't mean sickness will never touch us again this side of eternity, but it means the powers of the age to come are breaking into this age.

Think of healing like an overlap. In Eden, heaven and earth were one. Sin brought separation, along with death and disease. At the cross, Jesus bore our sicknesses and carried our pains (Isaiah 53:4). Now, when we pray for the sick, that future reality overlaps with the present moment. Heaven touches earth again.

When someone is healed, it is more than relief—it is revelation. It shows that Jesus is alive, that His Kingdom is real, and that He has authority over sickness. Healing is evangelistic. It

---

* NIV

opens hearts to the gospel. It reveals the King and His Kingdom.

The Compassion of the Healer

We must remember: healing is not about proving our power. It is about demonstrating His compassion. Again and again, the Gospels tell us that Jesus healed because He was moved with compassion (Matthew 14:14, Mark 1:41).

Healing flows from love. When you see someone suffering, you carry the heart of the Father who longs to restore them. Love is what moves you to step out and pray. Love is what keeps you from turning away in fear. Love is what ensures healing ministry never becomes mechanical or manipulative.

If you want to see more healings, don't start with technique —start with compassion. Ask God to let you feel His heart for the sick. When His love fills you, boldness follows.

The Five-Step Prayer Model

Healing is God's work, but He invites us to partner with Him. One helpful framework is the Five-Step Prayer Model, widely used in Spirit-filled churches. It's not a formula—it's a guide to help you pray with faith and love.

1. Interview

Ask simple questions: "What would you like prayer for?" "Where does it hurt?" This honors the person and helps you understand their need. Sometimes, the very act of listening with compassion opens the door for healing.

2. Diagnose

Ask the Holy Spirit: "What's going on here?" The Spirit may give insight into root causes—physical, emotional, or spiritual. Some sicknesses are purely physical. Others are tied to trauma, unforgiveness, or oppression. The Spirit helps you discern.

3. Prayer Selection

Decide how to pray. Sometimes you petition: "Lord, please heal this shoulder." Other times you command: "In Jesus' name, pain leave this shoulder." Sometimes you invite the Spirit: "Holy Spirit, come and fill this body." The key is to follow His leading.

4. Prayer Engagement

Lay hands if appropriate. Pray with faith, not striving. Short, simple prayers are often more effective than long, complicated ones. Pause and ask, "How are you feeling?" Repeat if necessary. Sometimes healing is instant; sometimes it's progressive.

5. Post-Prayer

Encourage the person. If they're healed, celebrate and give God glory. If they're partially healed, keep pressing in. If they're not healed yet, remind them they are loved, and God's presence is with them. Healing is never wasted—something always happens when we pray.

This model is not a rigid script, but it helps believers step out with confidence. The goal is not to perform, but to love well and release the Kingdom.

Testimonies That Multiply Faith

One of the most powerful ways to stir faith for healing is to share testimonies. Revelation 12:11 says we overcome by the blood of the Lamb and the word of our testimony. Testimonies remind us what God has done and prophesy what He wants to do again.

I remember praying for a man with chronic back pain. As we prayed, he felt heat in his spine and his pain disappeared. Later that week, he shared the testimony at a gathering. As he spoke, faith filled the room, and several others with back issues were healed without anyone even laying hands on them.

This is how the Kingdom multiplies. One healing sparks another. One testimony stirs another. The more we tell of His works, the more people believe—and the more heaven breaks in.

That's why it's important to document and share testimonies. Write them down. Tell them often. Let them create an atmosphere of expectation. In a greenhouse of testimonies, faith grows easily.

What About When Healing Doesn't Happen?

We must also acknowledge that not everyone we pray for is healed immediately. This tension can discourage us if we let it. But we must anchor ourselves in truth:

- Healing is in the atonement. Jesus bore our sicknesses (Isaiah 53:4).
- Healing is the will of God, revealed in Jesus. He never refused a sick person who came to Him.
- Healing is a process as well as a miracle. Sometimes it's instant. Sometimes it unfolds. Sometimes the healing comes in eternity.

Our job is obedience, not outcomes. We lay hands, we pray, we love. God does the healing. If someone isn't healed yet, we keep loving them, keep encouraging them, and keep believing.

Remember: faith is spelled R-I-S-K. If you never risk praying, you'll never see healing.

Practical Tips for Healing Ministry

1. Keep it simple. Don't overcomplicate. Pray short, clear prayers.
2. Partner with others. Healing often flows through teams. Invite others to join you.
3. Model compassion. Always honor the person. Never blame them if healing isn't immediate.
4. Expect God to move. Approach each prayer believing heaven wants to break in.
5. Celebrate progress. If pain goes from 8 to 4, rejoice and keep praying.
6. Stay humble. Healing is God's work, not yours. Always give Him glory.

Healing as Lifestyle, Not Event

Healing is not limited to the altar. It belongs in the grocery store, the workplace, the school, the neighborhood. The Spirit wants to heal through you in everyday life.

When you carry a greenhouse atmosphere, healing can happen anywhere. Your home becomes a place where sickness flees. Your workplace becomes a place where coworkers encounter the compassion of Jesus. Your city becomes a place where the Kingdom is advancing through ordinary believers who lay hands on the sick.

This is what Jesus envisioned when He said, "These signs will accompany those who believe." Not pastors only. Not evangelists only. Those who believe. That includes you.

Reflection Questions

1. How do you view healing—as optional or essential to the Kingdom?
2. What fears or doubts hold you back from praying for the sick?
3. Can you think of a time you experienced or witnessed healing? How did it impact your faith?
4. Who in your life right now needs healing? How can you step out to pray for them this week?
5. How could you create a culture of testimonies in your home, small group, or church?

Prayer

Lord Jesus, You are the same yesterday, today, and forever. You healed the sick when You walked the earth, and You heal the sick through Your people today. Fill me with compassion for the hurting. Give me boldness to step out in faith. Teach me to pray with simplicity and authority. Let healing flow through my hands as a sign of Your Kingdom's nearness. In Your name I pray, amen.

Declarations

- Healing is a sign of the Kingdom's nearness.
- I am a believer, and signs follow me.
- In Jesus' name, I lay hands on the sick and they recover.
- My prayers release the compassion of the Father.
- Testimonies multiply faith and breakthrough.
- Healing is my lifestyle, not just an event.

CHAPTER 12
AUTHORITY OVER DARKNESS: DELIVER US FROM EVIL

When Jesus taught His disciples how to pray, He included a line that many Christians skim past without much thought: "And lead us not into temptation, but deliver us from evil." (Matthew 6:13 NKJV).

This was not just a closing flourish to round out the prayer. It was a daily directive. Jesus was teaching His followers to pray continually for deliverance from the schemes of the enemy. Why? Because spiritual warfare is not an occasional event—it is the daily backdrop of the believer's life.

Paul echoes this in Ephesians 6:12: "For we do not wrestle against flesh and blood, but against principalities, against powers, against the rulers of the darkness of this age, against spiritual hosts of wickedness in the heavenly places."* The enemy is real. Demonic forces are real. But so is the authority of Christ in us. And that authority is greater.

Deliverance is not a fringe ministry for a select few. It is

---

* NKJV

normal Christianity. It is part of what it means to bring heaven to earth. Jesus said in Mark 16:17: "These signs will accompany those who believe: In my name they will cast out demons."* If you are a believer, this includes you.

The Normalcy of Deliverance

Many Christians think of deliverance as something dramatic, extreme, or only needed in rare cases. But if you read the Gospels, deliverance was woven into Jesus' everyday ministry. He preached, He healed, and He drove out demons. The crowds expected it.

When the kingdom of God comes near, darkness is exposed. Demons manifest because the light has entered the room. Deliverance is simply the enforcement of Christ's victory over the enemy.

In Luke 11:20, Jesus said, *"But if I cast out demons with the finger of God, surely the kingdom of God has come upon you."* † Deliverance is proof that the kingdom is advancing. It is not an embarrassing interruption—it is the King exercising His rule.

As believers, we must normalize deliverance again. It doesn't have to be sensational. It doesn't have to be chaotic. It can be gentle, Spirit-led, and full of peace.

The Armor of God

Paul tells us in Ephesians 6:10–18 to put on the whole armor of God so that we can stand against the enemy's schemes. This

---

* NIV
† NKJV

passage is not metaphorical poetry—it is practical instruction. Each piece of the armor represents a spiritual reality we must actively walk in.

- Belt of Truth. Truth holds everything together. Lies are the enemy's native language. When you embrace truth, you cut off his influence.
- Breastplate of Righteousness. Holiness guards your heart. Compromise leaves you exposed.
- Shoes of the Gospel of Peace. Everywhere you go, you carry the message of reconciliation. Peace disarms chaos.
- Shield of Faith. Faith extinguishes fiery darts of doubt, fear, and accusation.
- Helmet of Salvation. Salvation guards your mind. Your identity is secure in Christ.
- Sword of the Spirit. The Word of God is your offensive weapon. Declare it aloud.
- Prayer. Paul concludes with continual prayer in the Spirit. Prayer is how you wield the armor with power.

This armor is not something you "put on" once in a morning prayer and forget about. It is the lifestyle of a believer. To walk in truth, righteousness, peace, faith, salvation, the Word, and prayer is to walk armored. And when you are armored, the enemy's attacks cannot penetrate.

The Authority of the Believer

Authority is not based on volume or personality. It is based on position. You have authority over darkness because you are in Christ.

In Luke 10:19, Jesus told His disciples: *"I have given you authority to trample on snakes and scorpions and to overcome all the power of the enemy; nothing will harm you."** Notice that authority is given, not earned.

Authority flows from identity. When you know who you are —a son or daughter of the King—you act differently. You no longer plead with the devil. You command him. You no longer live in fear. You live in confidence.

Demons are not impressed by your shouting. They are not moved by your charisma. They are terrified of Christ in you. The same Spirit that raised Jesus from the dead dwells in you. When you speak in His name, darkness must obey.

Gentle Deliverance

Deliverance doesn't have to be dramatic. Yes, sometimes there are manifestations. But deliverance at its core is simple: discern, renounce, and command.

1. Discernment

Ask the Holy Spirit to show you what's happening. Sometimes the root is obvious—a spirit of fear, a spirit of infirmity, a spirit of addiction. Other times it requires listening for His whisper. Discernment is not suspicion; it is Spirit-led clarity.

2. Renunciation

Have the person verbally renounce the enemy's influ-

---

*   NIV

Agreement is powerful. When someone says, "I renounce the spirit of fear. I break agreement with lies," they are cutting ties with the enemy's claim.

3. Command

With gentleness and authority, command the spirit to leave in Jesus' name. You don't need long prayers. You don't need theatrics. A simple, "Spirit of fear, leave now in Jesus' name," is enough. The power is in His name, not in your performance.

Afterward, invite the Holy Spirit to fill the person. Deliverance is not just about eviction—it is about habitation. The goal is not an empty house, but a filled one.

Open Doors and Closing Them

Demons gain access through open doors. These can include:

- Unrepented sin. Habitual sin gives the enemy a foothold.
- Unforgiveness. Bitterness is a landing strip for torment.
- Occult involvement. Witchcraft, horoscopes, or occult practices open doors.
- Trauma and lies. Wounds can create agreements with the enemy's voice.

Deliverance involves closing these doors. Repentance, forgiveness, renunciation, and healing are essential. When the doors are closed, the enemy has no legal right to stay.

Deliverance as Ongoing Lifestyle

Jesus didn't just say, "Cast out demons once in a while." He taught us to pray daily: "Deliver us from evil." Deliverance is both an event and a lifestyle.

A lifestyle of deliverance means:

- Staying alert to lies and rejecting them quickly.
- Keeping short accounts with God and others.
- Filling your life with the Spirit through worship, Word, and prayer.
- Walking in community, where others can help you discern and stay free.

The goal is not just one-time freedom. The goal is to live free and help others do the same.

What Deliverance Reveals

Deliverance reveals the authority of the King. It shows that the kingdom of darkness has been defeated. It demonstrates that Jesus truly reigns.

Every time a demon flees, it testifies to the power of the cross. Colossians 2:15 says Jesus *"disarmed the rulers and authorities and put them to open shame, by triumphing over them in Him."** Deliverance is the public enforcement of that victory.

And it is not just about the individual being freed. Deliverance shifts atmospheres. Families change. Homes change. Cities change. When the people of God exercise their authority, entire regions can be transformed.

---

* ESV

Practical Guidelines for Deliverance Ministry

1. Always follow the Spirit. Don't rush, don't force. Listen to His leading.
2. Stay calm and gentle. Deliverance is not about volume. It's about authority.
3. Involve the person. Have them repent, renounce, and declare truth.
4. Protect dignity. Don't make a spectacle of someone's struggle.
5. Fill the house. Always pray for the Spirit to fill the person after deliverance.
6. Point to Jesus. Deliverance is not about demons—it's about the Deliverer.

Reflection Questions

1. How do you view deliverance—rare and extreme, or normal Christianity?
2. Are there any "open doors" in your life that the Spirit is highlighting?
3. What lies about yourself or God have you agreed with that need to be renounced?
4. How does the armor of God apply practically to your daily life?
5. Who in your sphere of influence might need freedom, and how could you step out to pray with them?

Prayer

Father, thank You that You have delivered me from the domain of darkness and transferred me into the kingdom of Your Son. I ask for discernment to recognize the enemy's schemes. I repent of compromise and close every open door. Fill me afresh with Your Spirit. Teach me to walk in Your authority with gentleness and boldness. Let freedom flow through my life to others. In Jesus' name, amen.

Declarations

- I put on the full armor of God daily.
- I walk in the authority of Jesus Christ over all the power of the enemy.
- I renounce every lie and agreement with darkness.
- The Holy Spirit fills me and empowers me to live free.
- Deliverance is normal Christianity, and it flows through me.
- Darkness must flee because the light of Christ lives in me.

CHAPTER 13

PROPHECY THAT BUILDS PEOPLE & PLACES

P aul tells us plainly in 1 Corinthians 14:1–3:

"Pursue love, and earnestly desire the spiritual gifts, especially that you may prophesy. For the one who speaks in a tongue speaks not to men but to God; for no one understands him, but he utters mysteries in the Spirit. On the other hand, the one who prophesies speaks to people for their upbuilding and encouragement and consolation."
ESV

Prophecy is not spooky. It is not reserved for a few elite voices. It is the natural overflow of the Spirit of God living within you and resting upon you. At its core, prophecy is about revealing the heart of the Father so that people and places are strengthened, encouraged, and comforted.

The God who tabernacled in Eden, who revealed Himself in the wilderness, and who made His home in Jesus has now made His home in you. That same Spirit longs to speak through you. Prophecy is the voice of heaven breaking into earth through surrendered sons and daughters.

Prophecy Is Rooted in Love

Notice that Paul begins this section by saying, "Pursue love, and earnestly desire the gifts." Love is the soil prophecy grows in. Without love, prophecy becomes empty noise. With love, prophecy becomes life-giving speech.

Prophecy is not about impressing others with how spiritual you are. It is about letting people hear, through your words, what the Father feels for them. When love is the motive, prophecy always points to Jesus and never to self.

Think about Jesus with the woman at the well in John 4. He revealed her story, but He did it in such a way that she was not shamed—she was restored. She left her jar, ran back to the town, and became an evangelist. Prophecy didn't expose her to condemn her. It revealed her to redeem her.

The Nature of Prophecy

Paul says prophecy is for upbuilding, encouragement, and consolation.

- Upbuilding. Prophecy strengthens the foundation of identity. It reminds people who they are and what they carry.
- Encouragement. Prophecy calls out courage in the weary. It gives strength to keep going.
- Consolation. Prophecy brings comfort to the hurting. It reminds them God sees, knows, and cares.

In short, prophecy builds people up, calls them forward, and heals their hearts. That is why prophecy is so desperately needed today. We live in a world tearing down identity, discouraging purpose, and wounding hearts. Prophecy reverses the curse by releasing heaven's words.

Prophecy and Identity

One of the most powerful effects of prophecy is the way it builds identity. When you speak what God says about someone, it anchors them in truth.

Jesus modeled this in John 1 when He met Simon. He said, "You are Simon son of John. You will be called Cephas" (which means Peter). Jesus prophesied Simon's identity as a rock long before Simon lived like one.

That is the nature of prophecy. It calls people not by their failures but by their future. It names them according to heaven's perspective, not earth's. It helps them see themselves through God's eyes. Prophecy is not flattery. It is not wishful thinking. It is truth revealed from heaven's vantage point. It is a kingly decree over someone's destiny.

Prophecy Points to Jesus

Revelation 19:10 says, *"The testimony of Jesus is the spirit of prophecy."** All true prophecy ultimately points to Jesus. If a prophetic word leads someone away from Christ, it is counterfeit.

Prophecy magnifies Jesus. It reveals His nature. It draws people closer to Him. Whether it is a word of encouragement,

---

* NKJV

direction, or comfort, prophecy should always increase intimacy with Christ.

This is important because prophecy is not about showing off secret knowledge. It is about revealing the heart of Jesus. If people leave a prophetic moment more impressed with you than with Him, something is off.

Prophecy and Places

Prophecy is not only for individuals—it is also for places. Throughout Scripture, God spoke destiny over cities and nations. He declared promises over regions. He announced His intentions for whole communities.

We see this with Nineveh, where Jonah's prophecy brought repentance and revival. We see it with Jerusalem, where prophets wept and spoke promises of restoration. Prophecy can shift atmospheres over neighborhoods, churches, and cities.

As believers, we carry authority not only to bless people but also to bless places. You can walk your neighborhood and declare God's purposes. You can prophesy life over your city. You can speak hope into dry regions. Prophecy is a tool for cultural transformation.

Growing in Prophecy

Paul told the Corinthians, "You can all prophesy one by one, so that all may learn and all be encouraged." (I Corinthians 14:31 ESV). This means prophecy is available to all believers. You may not stand in the office of a prophet, but you can function in the gift of prophecy.

So how do you grow?

1. Desire the gift. Ask God to use you prophetically. Hunger attracts heaven.
2. Learn to listen. Prophecy begins with hearing. Slow down. Tune your heart. Pay attention to impressions, thoughts, scriptures, or pictures that come.
3. Test and weigh. Not every impression is from God. Ask: Does this align with Scripture? Does it strengthen, encourage, or comfort? Does it point to Jesus?
4. Step out in faith. Prophecy requires risk. Share what you sense, humbly and simply. Trust God to use it.
5. Submit to community. Prophecy should be weighed by others. Accountability keeps the gift safe and healthy.

Activation: The 4 A's of Prophecy

Here is a simple framework to practice prophecy: the 4 A's.

- Ask. Ask the Holy Spirit for a word for someone.
- Attend. Pay attention to what comes—a picture, scripture, thought, or phrase.
- Articulate. Share it simply, without pressure. "I feel like the Lord may be saying..."
- Affirm. Let the other person affirm if it resonates. Humility leaves room for discernment.

This keeps prophecy grounded and approachable. You don't need to say, "Thus saith the Lord." You can simply share what you sense and let the Spirit confirm.

Prophecy and Agreement

Amos 3:3 NKJV asks, "*Can two walk together unless they are agreed?"* Prophecy helps bring people into agreement with heaven. God is not going to change His mind to walk with us. We must change our minds to walk with Him.

When we prophesy, we are releasing keys of the Kingdom. Jesus said in Matthew 16:19 NIV: *"I will give you the keys of the kingdom of heaven; whatever you bind on earth will be bound in heaven, and whatever you loose on earth will be loosed in heaven."*

The keys of the Kingdom are the ways of the Kingdom. Prophecy is one of those keys. It unlocks agreement. It aligns earth with heaven. It opens doors for God's purposes to flow.

Prophecy as Tabernacling Speech

Remember, God's desire has always been to dwell with His people. In Eden, heaven and earth overlapped. In Christ, the Word became flesh and tabernacled among us (John 1:14). Now we are the temple of the Spirit.

Prophecy is one of the ways heaven's speech flows through earthly vessels. When you prophesy, you are speaking as the dwelling place of God. His words find expression through your mouth. It is the tabernacling voice of God through His people.

This is why prophecy is weighty and holy. We are not playing with words. We are carrying the voice of heaven into the earth.

Creating Prophetic Culture

Prophecy flourishes in a culture of honor. When people feel safe, they are more likely to step out. When leaders create room for practice, the gift multiplies.

Practical steps for cultivating a prophetic culture:

- Share testimonies of prophetic words fulfilled.
- Encourage risk-taking in safe environments.
- Teach people how to weigh and test words.
- Celebrate encouragement, even if delivery is imperfect.
- Keep the focus on Jesus, not on prophetic celebrities.

A prophetic culture transforms a community. People feel seen, known, and called higher. Places become saturated with God's promises. Hope rises. Faith expands. The Kingdom advances.

Reflection Questions

1. How do you currently view prophecy—mystical and rare, or normal and accessible?
2. Have you ever received a prophetic word that impacted your identity or direction? How did it shape you?
3. In what ways could you begin practicing prophecy in your daily life?
4. How can you ensure your prophetic words always strengthen, encourage, and comfort?
5. What steps can you take to help build a prophetic culture in your family, small group, or church?

Prayer

Father, thank You for speaking to Your children. Thank You for the gift of prophecy that strengthens, encourages, and comforts. I ask You to tune my ears to Your voice and fill my heart with Your love. Teach me to step out in faith, to share humbly, and to always point people to Jesus. Use my words to build people and places for Your glory. In Jesus' name, amen.

Declarations

- I eagerly desire the gift of prophecy.
- God's voice flows through me to strengthen, encourage, and comfort.
- Prophecy builds identity and points people to Jesus.
- My words release heaven's agreement into earth.
- I will help cultivate a culture of prophetic encouragement in my community.
- Prophecy is normal Christianity, and I will walk in it.

CHAPTER 14

TONGUES & BOLDNESS: LANGUAGE OF FIRE

When the Holy Spirit was poured out in the upper room on the day of Pentecost, the first sign that erupted was tongues. *Acts 2:4 NIV says, "All of them were filled with the Holy Spirit and began to speak in other tongues as the Spirit enabled them."*

It is striking that the initial evidence of the Spirit's baptism was not healing, prophecy, or even miracles. It was speech. The Spirit released a new language—a language of fire—that marked the disciples as those who were not of this world.

Tongues remain one of the most misunderstood and neglected gifts in the church today. Some dismiss it as unnecessary. Others embrace it but rarely practice it. Yet Scripture shows us that praying in the Spirit is a key to living a strong, bold, and fruitful Christian life.

The Language of Heaven

Tongues are not random syllables or empty noise. They are Spirit-inspired utterances that bypass the mind and flow from the spirit. Paul explains in *1 Corinthians 14:14, "For if I pray in a tongue, my spirit prays, but my mind is unfruitful." ESV*

This means that tongues are the direct language of your inner man to God. When you pray in tongues, you are not limited by your vocabulary, your intellect, or even your understanding. The Spirit Himself intercedes through you. Romans 8:26–27 puts it this way:

"The Spirit helps us in our weakness. We do not know what we ought to pray for, but the Spirit Himself intercedes for us through wordless groans. And He who searches our hearts knows the mind of the Spirit, because the Spirit intercedes for God's people in accordance with the will of God." NIV

Tongues is heaven's way of bringing your prayers into perfect alignment with God's will. It is the Spirit bypassing the bottleneck of your mind and praying what needs to be prayed.

Building a Strong Spirit

One of the greatest benefits of tongues is how it builds the inner man. Jude 20 says, *"But you, beloved, building yourselves up on your most holy faith, praying in the Holy Spirit." NKJV*

To understand this, we need to grasp what it means to have a strong spirit. Your spirit is the core of your being—the part of you that connects with God, discerns truth, and governs your soul and body. When your spirit is weak, life's pressures crush you, temptations overwhelm you, and your emotions rule you. But when your spirit is strong, you can endure storms, resist temptation, discern clearly, and stand firm in faith.

A strong spirit sustains you when everything else feels

weak. Proverbs 18:14 says, *"The spirit of a man will sustain him in sickness, but a broken spirit who can bear?"** A strong spirit is like a fortress inside of you—it upholds your faith, keeps you steady, and enables you to walk in victory even when circumstances are against you.

Praying in tongues is one of God's primary ways of strengthening your spirit. Every time you pray in the Spirit, you are fortifying your inner man. You are charging yourself like a spiritual battery. You may not feel it immediately, but over time your resilience grows, your discernment sharpens, and your faith deepens.

This is why Paul said in *1 Corinthians 14:4 NKJV, "He who speaks in a tongue edifies himself."* The word "edifies" means to build up, like constructing a house or fortifying a wall. Tongues build you into a spiritual stronghold—a dwelling that is resistant to fear, doubt, and compromise.

Tongues and Boldness

Another fruit of tongues is boldness. *Acts 4:31 NKJV says, "After they prayed, the place where they were meeting was shaken. And they were all filled with the Holy Spirit and spoke the word of God boldly."*

Tongues and boldness go hand in hand. Why? Because tongues connect you to heaven's reality. They remind your spirit that you are seated with Christ in heavenly places (Eph. 2:6). When you pray in tongues, fear is displaced. Intimidation is broken. You step into a supernatural confidence that is not based on personality but on presence.

---

* NKJV

Boldness is not arrogance. Boldness is clarity, courage, and conviction rooted in the Spirit. It is the ability to stand in the face of opposition and declare the truth of Christ without shrinking back.

When Peter denied Jesus, he was timid and afraid. But after Pentecost, when tongues of fire rested on him, he stood before thousands and boldly declared the gospel. The difference was not Peter's willpower. It was the filling of the Spirit, released through the language of fire.

Removing Fear

Tongues dismantle fear. Fear is often rooted in the mind— the endless "what if" scenarios that paralyze us. But when you pray in tongues, you bypass the mind. You step into the Spirit, where perfect love casts out fear.

Fear says, "You can't."
Tongues reminds you, "God can."
Fear says, "You're alone."
Tongues reminds you, "The Spirit is interceding for you."
Fear says, "You don't know what to pray."
Tongues reminds you, "The Spirit is praying through you."

As you pray in tongues daily, fear loses its grip. Your spirit rises above the chatter of anxiety and steps into faith. You begin to live with a confidence that no matter what happens, heaven is backing you up.

Tongues Fuel Mission

The language of fire was given on the day of Pentecost not for private enjoyment but for public mission. When the disciples spoke in tongues, the nations gathered in Jerusalem heard the wonders of God declared in their own languages. Tongues announced the global mission of the gospel. Tongues fuel mission in two ways:

1. Empowering you personally. Tongues fill you with boldness to share your faith. They strengthen your inner man so that you are not easily shaken. They keep you aligned with the Spirit as you go about your day.
2. Releasing heaven corporately. Tongues create an atmosphere where the Spirit moves. When a church prays in tongues together, faith rises, unity deepens, and boldness spreads. It is like stoking a fire until it blazes into revival.

Tongues are not meant to be hidden in a corner. They are meant to propel the church outward in power.

Daily Habit of Tongues

If tongues build a strong spirit, remove fear, and fuel mission, then we should treat them as a daily habit, not an occasional experience. Here are practical ways to cultivate tongues in your daily life:

- Start your day in tongues. Before you check your phone or face your to-do list, spend 10–15 minutes praying in the Spirit. It aligns your heart with heaven before the noise of the world hits.
- Pray in tongues while driving. Turn your commute into a sanctuary.

- Use tongues in intercession. When you don't know how to pray for someone, let the Spirit pray through you.
- Pray in tongues before ministry. Whether you're preaching, leading worship, or serving, tongues prepare your spirit for boldness and clarity.
- End your day in tongues. Release the worries of the day and enter rest with your spirit fortified.

1 Corinthians 14:4, "He who speaks in a tongue edifies himself." NKJV

Over time, these daily deposits build a reservoir of strength. Your spirit becomes resilient, alert, and courageous.

Common Misunderstandings

Some believers hesitate with tongues because of misunderstandings. Let's address a few:

- "Tongues are not for today." Scripture never says the gift has ceased. In fact, Paul said, *"Do not forbid speaking in tongues"* (1 Cor. 14:39).
- "Tongues are weird." What's truly strange is a powerless Christianity. Tongues are a supernatural gift from a supernatural God.
- "I don't feel anything when I pray in tongues." Tongues are not about feelings. They are about faith. Even if your mind feels unfruitful, your spirit is being built up.
- "I don't know if I'm doing it right." Tongues are not about performance. If the Spirit has given you utterance, trust Him. Start small, and let the flow grow.

Reflection Questions

1. How often do you pray in tongues, and how could you make it a daily habit?
2. Do you view tongues as optional, or as essential for building a strong spirit?
3. Where in your life do you need greater boldness right now?
4. How might tongues help you step past fear into mission?
5. What atmosphere would shift in your home or church if praying in the Spirit became normal?

Prayer

Holy Spirit, thank You for the gift of tongues. Thank You for giving me a language of fire that builds my inner man, removes fear, and fuels mission. I ask You to stir up this gift in me. Teach me to make praying in the Spirit a daily habit. Fill me with boldness to proclaim Jesus without fear. Strengthen my spirit so I can stand firm in every season. Let Your fire burn in me and through me. In Jesus' name, amen.

Declarations

- I build up my spirit daily by praying in tongues.
- My spirit is strong, resilient, and anchored in Christ.
- Fear has no hold on me; I walk in boldness.
- My words release heaven's fire into the earth.
- Tongues fuel my mission and align me with God's will.
- I carry the language of heaven everywhere I go.

CHAPTER 15
THE GREAT CO-MISSION:
MAKE DISCIPLES, NOT SPECTATORS

W hen Jesus rose from the dead, He did not leave His disciples with vague instructions. He gave them what has become known as the Great Commission:

"All authority in heaven and on earth has been given to Me. Therefore, go and make disciples of all nations, baptizing them in the name of the Father and of the Son and of the Holy Spirit, and teaching them to obey everything I have commanded you. And surely I am with you always, to the very end of the age." (Matthew 28:18–20 NIV)

This is the mission statement of the Church. It is not optional. It is not reserved for a few. It is the assignment of every believer. The purpose of kingdom power is not to put on a show, impress a crowd, or create religious celebrities. The purpose of kingdom power is to make disciples.

The Great Commission is not about making converts or gathering spectators. It is about raising sons and daughters who are formed into the likeness of Christ, equipped to carry His kingdom, and empowered to multiply His mission.

All Authority, All Nations

The Commission begins with authority: *"All authority in heaven and on earth has been given to Me."* Jesus is not commissioning us out of our own strength. He is sending us out under His authority.

Because all authority belongs to Him, no place is off limits. No nation is unreachable. No neighborhood is too hard. No person is too far gone. His authority covers the whole earth.

The scope of the mission is also clear: "Go and make disciples of all nations." The gospel is not a private religion or a tribal belief. It is good news for every people, every culture, every tongue. God's heart is global, and so must ours be.

Discipleship, Not Decisions

Notice that Jesus did not say, "Go and get people to raise their hand at an altar call." He said, "Go and make disciples."

A disciple is not someone who simply believes in Jesus. A disciple is someone who follows Him, obeys Him, and learns to live as He lived. Discipleship is a lifelong process of transformation.

Too often the church has settled for decisions instead of discipleship. We count how many prayed a prayer but fail to ask how many are walking with Jesus. But the kingdom mandate is not to gather a crowd of spectators. It is to form a family of disciples.

The Rhythm of Discipleship

Jesus outlined a clear rhythm for making disciples:

1. Preach the gospel with clarity. The good news must be declared. People cannot follow a Jesus they do not know.
2. Baptize. Baptism is the entrance into a new family and a new way of life. It is not optional—it is obedience.
3. Teach obedience. Discipleship is not merely transferring knowledge. It is teaching people to obey everything Jesus commanded.

These three elements—gospel clarity, baptism, and obedience—are the backbone of discipleship. Without them, the church produces consumers, not disciples.

Gospel Clarity

At the heart of the Great Commission is the message of the gospel. We cannot make disciples if the message is muddled. The gospel is not self-help. It is not moral improvement. It is not motivational speaking.

The gospel is this: Jesus Christ, the Son of God, died for our sins, was buried, rose on the third day, and now reigns as Lord. Through Him, we are forgiven, reconciled to God, and given new life in the Spirit.

Paul said in *Romans 1:16 NIV, "I am not ashamed of the gospel, because it is the power of God that brings salvation to everyone who believes."* The power is not in our presentation. The power is in the message itself.

We must be clear, simple, and bold in proclaiming the

gospel. When the gospel is proclaimed with clarity, the Spirit confirms it with power.

Baptism: Marked by the Kingdom

Baptism is more than a ritual. It is a burial and a resurrection. *Romans 6:4 says, "We were therefore buried with Him through baptism into death in order that, just as Christ was raised from the dead through the glory of the Father, we too may live a new life."*

Through baptism, a person identifies with Jesus' death and resurrection. They die to the old life and rise to the new. They are marked as citizens of a new kingdom.

Baptism is also communal. You are baptized not just into Christ but into His body. You join a family. Discipleship is never a solo journey. It is always lived in community.

If you want to see disciples multiplied, make baptism central. Celebrate it often. Teach its meaning. Let people see the joy of new life as others go under the water and come out transformed.

Teaching Obedience

The final component of the Great Commission is teaching obedience. Jesus said, "Teach them to obey everything I have commanded you."

Notice He did not say, "Teach them everything I commanded you." He said, "Teach them to obey." The focus is not information but formation. Discipleship is about obedience.

Obedience is the fruit of love. Jesus said, *"If you love Me, keep My commandments" (John 14:15 NKJV)*. Teaching obedience means helping people not just know what Jesus said but live it out. It means walking with them, modeling it, and holding them accountable.

The Oikos Map: Reaching Your Relational Network

One of the most practical tools for disciple-making is what some call an "Oikos map." The Greek word oikos means "household" or "network of relationships." It refers to the people already in your sphere of influence—family, friends, neighbors, coworkers.

Jesus often worked through oikos networks. The Samaritan woman brought her whole town. The Philippian jailer and his household were baptized. Lydia's household became a hub for the gospel.

Creating an Oikos map is simple:

1. Write down the names of people in your relational network who do not yet follow Jesus.
2. Pray for them daily.
3. Look for opportunities to serve, share, and invite them.
4. When they respond, disciple them in community.

This shifts evangelism from a program to a lifestyle. It reminds you that your mission field starts where you already have relationship.

Power for Discipleship

Remember, the Great Commission begins with authority

and ends with presence: "Surely I am with you always." Discipleship is not a human endeavor. It is fueled by the Spirit's power.

Acts 1:8 NLT says, *"You will receive power when the Holy Spirit comes upon you; and you will be My witnesses in Jerusalem, and in all Judea and Samaria, and to the ends of the earth."*

The Spirit within transforms you. The Spirit upon empowers you. Both are necessary for discipleship. Transformation makes you a disciple. Power makes you a disciplemaker.

This is why the gifts of the Spirit—healing, prophecy, tongues, deliverance—are not side issues. They are tools for discipleship. They reveal the reality of the kingdom so that people follow Jesus not just in word but in power.

Disciples, Not Spectators

One of the greatest tragedies in the church today is the number of spectators. People attend services, sing songs, and listen to sermons, but never step into mission. They watch a few do ministry instead of realizing ministry is for all.

The Great Commission leaves no room for spectators. Every believer is called to make disciples. Every believer has an oikos. Every believer has the Spirit. Every believer has authority in Christ. When the church shifts from spectator to disciplemaker, the world will be turned upside down again.

Multiplication, Not Maintenance

The goal of discipleship is multiplication, not maintenance.

Jesus said, "Go and make disciples of all nations." He was not envisioning a church that merely maintains believers. He was envisioning a movement that multiplies disciples.

Multiplication happens when disciples make disciples who make disciples. It is exponential growth, not just addition. It is the kingdom spreading like yeast through dough or like a seed growing into a tree. This is why small, reproducible patterns are so important. Complicated systems don't multiply. Simple obedience does.

Reflection Questions

1. Do you see yourself as someone called to make disciples, or have you slipped into being a spectator?
2. How clear is your grasp of the gospel? Could you explain it simply to someone in your oikos?
3. What role does baptism play in your understanding of discipleship?
4. How can you practically begin teaching obedience to those around you?
5. Who are 3–5 people in your oikos that you could begin praying for and discipling?

Prayer

Father, thank You for entrusting me with the Great Commission. Thank You that I am called not just to follow Jesus but to make disciples. Fill me with boldness to proclaim the gospel with clarity. Help me to walk in obedience so I can model it for others. Open my eyes to my oikos—the people You've already placed around me. Empower me by Your Spirit to multiply disciples until the nations are filled with Your glory. In Jesus' name, amen.

Declarations

- I am commissioned by Jesus to make disciples of all nations.
- The gospel I carry is clear, powerful, and life-changing.
- Baptism marks new believers into a family and a new life.
- I teach others to obey Jesus, not just to know about Him.
- My oikos is my mission field, and I will steward it faithfully.
- I am not a spectator; I am a disciple-maker.

CONCLUSION
UNTIL THE WHOLE EARTH LOOKS LIKE HEAVEN

The story of Scripture begins in a garden and ends in a city. But the theme is the same: heaven and earth as one, God dwelling with His people. Genesis shows us Eden—God walking with man in the cool of the day, His space and our space overlapping without separation. Revelation shows us the New Jerusalem—no temple needed because *"the dwelling of God is with man" (Rev. 21:3 ESV)*. The beginning and the end harmonize. What was lost through sin is restored through Christ.

This has always been God's intent. Not escape. Not delay. Not boredom. But union. Heaven and earth one again.

When Isaiah cried out, *"Oh, that You would rend the heavens and come down" (Isa. 64:1 NKJV)*, he was longing for this union to be restored. When Jesus stepped into the waters of baptism and the heavens were torn open, that cry began to be fulfilled. When He hung on the cross and the veil was torn in two, the separation was abolished. When the Spirit filled the upper room, the kingdom came rushing in.

And now, as the Church, we live in that overlap. We are not waiting for one day to finally experience the presence of God. The Spirit is already within us. The Spirit is already upon us. The heavens are already open over us. We are carriers of the New Eden.

The Kingdom Vision

The vision of this book has been simple but bold: stop living as if the heavens are closed. Stop settling for a boring Christianity that reduces salvation to waiting for heaven. Stop measuring your life by how much sin you avoided or how faithfully you endured. Instead, lift your eyes to the purpose and power God has entrusted to you.

- You were made to host His presence like Eden.
- You were made to walk as a living tabernacle of His Spirit.
- You were made to heal the sick, cast out demons, prophesy, and make disciples.
- You were made to live as a greenhouse where heaven touches earth.

When you live this way, Christianity is anything but boring. It is vibrant, dangerous, exhilarating, and deeply fulfilling. It is the life God designed for His sons and daughters.

From Homes → Hubs → Cities → Nations

The kingdom does not advance by skipping steps. It begins in the smallest places and grows outward. Jesus compared it to yeast working through dough or a mustard seed becoming a tree. It starts small but does not stay small.

It begins in homes. Your house can be an outpost of heaven. When you consecrate your home, cleanse its atmosphere, and welcome the Spirit daily, it becomes a greenhouse for God's presence. Children grow up knowing the nearness of God. Guests walk in and sense peace. Prayer, worship, and the Word saturate the atmosphere. Your home becomes Eden again.

It grows into hubs. As households host the presence, they gather into communities—small groups, house churches, prayer hubs, and local congregations. These hubs multiply the presence. They become wells of healing, deliverance, and discipleship. They are outposts of the kingdom in neighborhoods and towns.

It impacts cities. As hubs multiply, cities begin to change. Darkness is pushed back. Culture is transformed. The oppressed find freedom. The poor find hope. Leaders are discipled. Businesses, schools, and governments feel the ripple effect of the kingdom.

It spreads to nations. The endgame of the Great Commission is nations discipled. Not just individuals, not just gatherings, but whole cultures transformed by the presence of God. Revelation 11:15 declares, *"The kingdoms of this world have become the kingdom of our Lord and of His Christ, and He will reign forever and ever."**That is where the story is headed—until the whole earth looks like heaven.

Guard the Flame Within

If you want to live as a carrier of this vision, you must guard the flame within. Paul told Timothy, *"Fan into flame the gift of*

---

* NKJV

God, which is in you" (2 Tim. 1:6 NIV). The Spirit within you is
your lifeline. He convicts, comforts, teaches, and transforms.
He shapes you into the likeness of Christ.

Guarding the flame means choosing holiness over compromise, intimacy over distraction, obedience over comfort. It
means refusing to let sin grieve Him or cynicism quench Him.
It means setting your attention and affection on Jesus daily.

Without the flame within, power becomes dangerous.
Without intimacy, ministry becomes hollow. Guard the flame
so that your inner life is a true reflection of heaven's culture.

Release the River Upon

Jesus said in John 7:38, *"Whoever believes in Me, as Scripture
has said, rivers of living water will flow from within them."** This
He spoke of the Spirit who would be poured out.

The Spirit is not just within you for your benefit. He is upon
you for the world's benefit. The river of living water is meant to
flow out. Healing, deliverance, prophecy, boldness—these are
rivers for others to drink.

Release the river. Don't dam it up. Don't keep it to yourself.
Step out in faith. Pray for the sick. Speak what God shows you.
Share the gospel with courage. Let heaven flow through you
into the earth.

When the flame within fuels the river upon, the kingdom is
released in power.

---

*   NIV

Carriers of the New Eden

In Revelation 21, John saw a vision of the New Jerusalem descending from heaven. He noticed something striking: *"I did not see a temple in the city, because the Lord God Almighty and the Lamb are its temple" (Rev. 21:22 NIV).*

Why no temple? Because heaven and earth are one again. God's dwelling is no longer confined to a building. His people are His dwelling. His presence fills everything.

That is the trajectory of history. And you are called to be a forerunner of it now. As a believer, you are already a carrier of the New Eden. You host God's presence in your body, your home, your community. Wherever you go, the overlap of heaven and earth goes with you.

The world is not waiting for a church that hides until the rapture. The world is waiting for a church that carries the glory of the New Eden into every sphere of life.

A Final Charge

So here is the charge:

- Guard the flame within. Don't let sin, apathy, or distraction snuff it out.
- Release the river upon. Let boldness, gifts, and power flow through you.
- Live as a carrier of the New Eden. Let your life be a preview of heaven on earth.

If you do, your home will change. Your city will change.

Nations will change. And you will discover that Christianity is not boring—it is breathtaking.

The heavens are open. The veil is torn. The Spirit is given. The kingdom is advancing. Until the whole earth looks like heaven.

Reflection Questions

1. How does the Eden-to-New Jerusalem storyline reshape your understanding of God's intent for earth?
2. In what practical ways can your home become a greenhouse of God's presence?
3. What steps can you take to guard the flame of the Spirit within you?
4. Where is God calling you to release the river of His Spirit upon others?
5. How could your oikos, your hub, or your city look different if heaven invaded it through you?

Prayer

Father, thank You that from the beginning to the end, Your desire has been to dwell with us. Thank You for tearing the veil, opening the heavens, and sending Your Spirit. I consecrate myself to You again. Help me to guard the flame within and release the river upon. Make my home, my community, and my city a place where heaven touches earth. Let my life be a preview of the New Eden until the day when You dwell with us fully and forever. In Jesus' name, amen.

Declarations

- I live under an open heaven; the veil is torn.
- My body is the temple of the Holy Spirit.
- I guard the flame within through holiness and intimacy.
- I release the river upon through boldness and power.
- My home is a greenhouse of God's presence.
- I am a carrier of the New Eden until the whole earth looks like heaven.

APPENDIX A

30-DAY OPEN-HEAVEN ACTIVATION PLAN

How to Use This Plan

- Set aside 15–20 minutes daily.
- Read the Scripture slowly.
- Pray the prayer prompt out loud.
- Take one simple obedience step.
- Record your testimony—what you felt, heard, or saw.

Week 1 — Awareness of His Presence

Focus: Becoming conscious of God's nearness.
Day 1

- Scripture: Psalm 16:11
- Prayer: "Lord, make me aware of Your presence today."
- Obedience: Take 5 minutes of silence, no phone, no distractions.
- Testimony: _____

Day 2

- Scripture: Exodus 33:14
- Prayer: "Your presence goes with me; give me rest."
- Obedience: Before every task, whisper: "You're with me."
- Testimony: _____

Day 3

- Scripture: John 14:23
- Prayer: "Father, make my heart Your dwelling place."
- Obedience: Welcome Him audibly into each room of your house.
- Testimony: _____

Day 4

- Scripture: Matthew 28:20
- Prayer: "Jesus, thank You that You are with me always."
- Obedience: Write three moments you noticed Him today.
- Testimony: _____

Day 5

- Scripture: Psalm 27:4
- Prayer: "Give me one desire: to gaze on Your beauty."
- Obedience: Spend 10 minutes in worship without asking for anything.
- Testimony: _____

Day 6

- Scripture: Hebrews 13:5
- Prayer: "You will never leave me or forsake me."
- Obedience: Replace one fear-thought with this promise today.
- Testimony: _____

Day 7

- Scripture: Isaiah 41:10
- Prayer: "I will not fear, for You are with me."
- Obedience: Encourage one person with God's nearness.
- Testimony: _____

Week 2 — Identity in Christ

Focus: Living as sons and daughters, not orphans.
Day 8

- Scripture: Romans 8:15
- Prayer: "Abba, remind me I am Your child."
- Obedience: Write down lies you've believed about identity. Cross them out.
- Testimony: _____

Day 9

- Scripture: Galatians 4:7
- Prayer: "Thank You that I am no longer a slave but an heir."
- Obedience: Journal 3 ways you see God's favor in your life.
- Testimony: _____

Day 10

- Scripture: 2 Corinthians 5:17
- Prayer: "I am a new creation in Christ."
- Obedience: Declare this truth 5 times throughout the day.
- Testimony: _____

Day 11

- Scripture: John 1:12
- Prayer: "I have the right to be called a child of God."
- Obedience: Share this verse with a friend or family member.
- Testimony: _____

Day 12

- Scripture: Ephesians 1:5
- Prayer: "I am adopted in love through Christ."
- Obedience: Write a gratitude letter to God for adopting you.
- Testimony: _____

Day 13

- Scripture: Colossians 1:13
- Prayer: "You rescued me from darkness into the kingdom of Your Son."
- Obedience: Turn off one "darkness" influence (TV, music, etc.) today.
- Testimony: _____

Day 14

- Scripture: 1 Peter 2:9
- Prayer: "I am chosen, royal, holy, and called."
- Obedience: Declare this identity over yourself in the mirror.
- Testimony: _____

Week 3 — Release of the Kingdom

Focus: Letting heaven flow outward.
Day 15

- Scripture: Acts 1:8
- Prayer: "Clothe me with power for witness."
- Obedience: Share one testimony of God's goodness with someone.
- Testimony: _____

Day 16

- Scripture: Matthew 10:8
- Prayer: "Freely I've received; freely I give."
- Obedience: Pray for someone's healing.
- Testimony: _____

Day 17

- Scripture: Luke 10:19
- Prayer: "Thank You for authority over darkness."
- Obedience: Pray over your home, commanding fear to leave.
- Testimony: _____

Day 18

- Scripture: John 7:38
- Prayer: "Let rivers of living water flow from me."
- Obedience: Speak encouragement over someone discouraged.
- Testimony: _____

Day 19

- Scripture: 1 Corinthians 12:7
- Prayer: "Manifest Your Spirit through me today."
- Obedience: Ask God for a word of encouragement for someone. Share it.
- Testimony: _____

Day 20

- Scripture: Mark 16:17–18
- Prayer: "I am a believer; signs will follow me."
- Obedience: Pray boldly for someone outside church.
- Testimony: _____

Day 21

- Scripture: Romans 14:17
- Prayer: "Let righteousness, peace, and joy overflow through me."
- Obedience: Bring peace into one tense situation today.
- Testimony: _____

Week 4 — Multiplication of Mission

Focus: Making disciples, not spectators.

Day 22

- Scripture: Matthew 28:19–20
- Prayer: "Send me to make disciples."
- Obedience: Write down your oikos map (relational network).
- Testimony: _____

Day 23

- Scripture: Acts 2:42
- Prayer: "Make me devoted to teaching, fellowship, breaking bread, and prayer."
- Obedience: Invite someone into a meal + prayer.
- Testimony: _____

Day 24

- Scripture: 2 Timothy 2:2
- Prayer: "Help me entrust truth to faithful people who multiply."
- Obedience: Share one Scripture with a younger believer.
- Testimony: _____

Day 25

- Scripture: Colossians 1:28
- Prayer: "Help me proclaim Christ and present others mature."
- Obedience: Encourage a believer to take a next step of obedience.
- Testimony: _____

Day 26

- Scripture: John 20:21
- Prayer: "As the Father sent Jesus, send me."
- Obedience: Pray about one specific mission God is giving you.
- Testimony: _____

Day 27

- Scripture: Philippians 1:5
- Prayer: "Make me a partner in the gospel."
- Obedience: Support a missionary or kingdom cause financially.
- Testimony: _____

Day 28

- Scripture: Acts 13:2
- Prayer: "Speak, Lord, and send me where You will."
- Obedience: Fast one meal and ask God to show you your next step.
- Testimony: _____

Day 29

- Scripture: Habakkuk 2:14
- Prayer: "Fill the earth with Your glory through me."
- Obedience: Share the gospel with one person today.
- Testimony: _____=

Day 30

- Scripture: Revelation 21:3
- Prayer: "Make me a carrier of the New Eden."
- Obedience: Write a declaration of how you will live from this day forward.
- Testimony: _____

APPENDIX B
HOME CONSECRATION & CLEANSING LITURGY

Your home is more than walls and furniture—it is an atmosphere. Scripture shows us that places can be consecrated (set apart for God's glory) or contaminated (opened to fear, sin, or darkness). God's desire has always been to tabernacle with His people—not in tents or temples made with human hands, but in dwelling places He has chosen. That includes you and your home.

When you consecrate your home, you are making it a greenhouse of the kingdom—a place where God's presence is hosted, His peace rules, and His power flows.

Step 1: Dedication (Ownership Transfer)

The first step is to clearly declare that your home belongs to God.

Scripture: *"As for me and my house, we will serve the Lord." (Joshua 24:15 NIV)*

Prayer:

"Father, in the name of Jesus, I dedicate this home to You. Every wall, every room, every corner belongs to You. This is not just my dwelling —it is Your dwelling. May Your presence fill this place. May Your glory rest here. I declare that this home will serve the Lord in all things."

Action:

- Walk through your front door with oil (olive oil works fine) and mark the doorframe with the sign of the cross.
- Declare out loud: "This house belongs to Jesus Christ."

Step 2: Cleansing (Removing Contamination)

Just as Israel removed idols from their land before God's glory filled the temple, we remove anything in our homes that grieves or quenches the Spirit.

Scripture: *"Get rid of the foreign gods you have with you, and purify yourselves and change your clothes." (Genesis 35:2 NIV)*

Prayer:

"Holy Spirit, reveal anything in this home that does not honor You. Show me objects, media, habits, or influences that open the door to darkness. Give me courage to remove them."

Action:

- Go room by room. Pause and listen.

- Remove or destroy anything the Spirit highlights (occult symbols, certain media, unhealthy decorations, books, music, even lingering unforgiveness or conflict).
- Pray in each room: "In Jesus' name, I command every spirit not of God to leave this space now. This room is cleansed by the blood of Jesus."

Step 3: Blessing (Inviting God's Atmosphere)

Cleansing removes what shouldn't be there; blessing invites what should.

Scripture: *"The LORD bless you and keep you; the LORD make His face shine on you and be gracious to you; the LORD turn His face toward you and give you peace." (Numbers 6:24–26 NLT)*

Prayer & Action (Room-by-Room):

- Living Room: "Lord, fill this place with joy, hospitality, and worship. May conversations here glorify You."
- Kitchen/Dining: "Bless this table. Let meals shared here be full of gratitude, laughter, and fellowship."
- Bedrooms: "Let these rooms be filled with peace and rest. May dreams be holy, and hearts be guarded."
- Bathrooms: "Lord, let these be places of cleansing, refreshing, and renewal of body and soul."
- Work/Study Spaces: "Bless these rooms with wisdom, creativity, and revelation. May everything produced here honor You."
- Entryways/Doors: "Father, may every person who enters encounter Your presence. Guard this threshold from harm."

Step 4: Communion (Sealing the Covenant)

Taking communion in your home is a powerful act of covenant renewal, declaring your household under the blood of Jesus.

Scripture: *"But as often as you eat this bread and drink this cup, you proclaim the Lord's death till He comes."* (1 Corinthians 11:26)

Prayer:

"Jesus, thank You for Your body and blood shed for me. As I take communion, I declare that this home is under Your covenant protection. Your blood covers every doorway, every window, and every person here."

Action:

- Share bread and juice/wine with family or friends.
- Declare together: "This home is sealed in the covenant of Christ."

Step 5: Ongoing Atmosphere Shifts

Consecration is not a one-time event—it is a lifestyle. Atmosphere is shaped by what we continually allow or disallow.

Practices to Maintain the Atmosphere:

- Play worship music often.
- Read Scripture out loud in your home.
- Begin family or personal days with prayer.

- Keep short accounts—repent quickly, forgive quickly.
- Regularly pray the Lord's Prayer (Matt. 6:9–13) over your household.

Optional: Family/Group Declaration

Stand together in your living room and declare aloud:

"We declare this home is the dwelling place of the Most High God. Jesus Christ is Lord over every room, every person, and every activity. The Spirit of God fills this house with peace, joy, healing, and freedom. We renounce every work of darkness and welcome the kingdom of light. From this day forward, this home will be a greenhouse of heaven, a sanctuary of His presence, and a beacon of His glory. In Jesus' name, amen."

APPENDIX C
HEALING & DELIVERANCE QUICK CARDS

These quick cards are designed to give you confidence as you minister. They don't replace relationship with the Holy Spirit—He is always the leader—but they provide a clear, biblical flow so you won't get stuck.

Healing Quick Card

Mark 16:17–18; James 5:14–15
1. Connect

- Ask: "Where is the pain? How long have you had it?"
- Listen with compassion. Don't rush.

2. Invite the Spirit

- Prayer: "Come, Holy Spirit."
- Sometimes healing happens here before you even pray further.

3. Command Healing

- Pray with authority, not begging.
- Example: "In Jesus' name, I command this [back/knee/headache/etc.] to be healed right now. Pain, leave. Body, be restored."

4. Check Progress

- Ask: "Do you notice anything changing?"
- Celebrate every improvement, even partial. Pray again if needed.

5. Minister Love

- Encourage them: healing is an expression of God's love, not a performance.
- Example: "Jesus is showing His love for you today."

6. Release & Follow-Up

- Tell them: "Keep thanking God for what He's done."
- If they're part of your church, encourage them to testify next time.

Deliverance Quick Card

Luke 10:19; Matthew 6:13; Acts 16:18
1. Discern the Issue

- Common signs: torment, fear, addiction, oppression, recurring nightmares.
- Ask: "When did this begin?" Often points to an open door.

2. Lead in Repentance & Renunciation

- Example prayer: "Jesus, I repent for opening the door to [fear, bitterness, occult, immorality]. I renounce every agreement I made with darkness. I break its power in Jesus' name."

3. Command the Spirit to Leave

- Pray calmly but firmly.
- Example: "In the name of Jesus Christ, I command every unclean spirit of [fear, torment, addiction] to leave right now. You have no authority here."

4. Invite the Holy Spirit to Fill

- After deliverance, always pray for infilling.
- Example: "Holy Spirit, fill every place that was emptied. Bring peace, joy, and righteousness."

5. Ground in Truth & Community

- Give them Scripture promises to stand on (Romans 8:1, 2 Timothy 1:7, James 4:7).
- Encourage them to stay connected in community and resist isolation.

Safety & Love Guidelines

- Always minister with love. Healing and deliverance flow from compassion, not performance.
- Respect the person's dignity. Keep it calm, not dramatic. Never shame, expose, or force.
- Stay Spirit-led. If you don't sense God's direction, pause and pray silently.

- Use a team when possible. Two or more provide safety, accountability, and balance.
- Don't minister alone to the opposite sex. Always have another trusted person present.
- Celebrate progress, not perfection. Sometimes freedom and healing come in layers.

Sample Declarations for Healing & Deliverance

- *"By His stripes I am healed." (Isaiah 53:5)*
- *"The Spirit of Him who raised Jesus from the dead gives life to my body." (Romans 8:11)*
- *"God has not given me a spirit of fear, but of power, love, and a sound mind." (2 Timothy 1:7)*
- *"Greater is He who is in me than he who is in the world." (1 John 4:4)*

APPENDIX D

LEADER'S GUIDE FOR SMALL GROUPS / CLASSES

This guide is designed to help you lead others through The Purpose and Power of the Believer on Earth. The goal is not information only, but activation: to form disciples who carry heaven's culture into homes, hubs, cities, and nations.

How to Use This Guide

- Gather weekly. 60–90 minutes is ideal.
- Assign reading. Each week's chapter(s) should be read beforehand.
- Open with prayer. Welcome the Spirit's leadership.
- Discuss & share. Use the Reflection Questions at the end of each chapter.
- Activate. Every session includes a practical exercise.
- Close with prayer & testimony. Encourage participants to bring back stories each week.

12-Week Flow

Week 1: Introduction — Why This Book, Why Now

- Reading: Introduction.
- Focus: Moving from boring Christianity to a life of purpose, presence, and power.
- Discussion: What excites you most about living under an open heaven?
- Activation: Each person writes a one-sentence expectation prayer for the 12 weeks.

Weeks 2–4: Part I — The Kingdom Now (Chs. 1–3)

Week 2: Chapter 1 — Your Father's Good Pleasure

- Focus: The kingdom is God's gift, now and in fullness.
- Discussion: How do you pray differently when you see "on earth as in heaven" as a mandate?
- Activation: Pray the Lord's Prayer slowly together, pausing after each section to add personal prayers.

Week 3: Chapter 2 — The Great Unveiling

- Focus: Rended heavens, rended veil, God's intent for heaven and earth as one.
- Discussion: How do you see your life as a temple where God dwells?
- Activation: Walk your meeting space together, dedicating it as a "greenhouse" for His presence.

Week 4: Chapter 3 — Royal Search

- Focus: Kings search out mysteries; keys of the kingdom unlock heaven.
- Discussion: Share one "mystery" God has revealed to you that shifted your walk.

- Activation: Practice the "Scripture Listening" method on one short passage.

Weeks 5–7: Part II — Spirit Within & Upon (Chs. 4–6)

Week 5: Chapter 4 — The Spirit Within

- Focus: New heart, fruit of the Spirit, holiness.
- Discussion: Which fruit of the Spirit do you want to see more of in your life?
- Activation: Do a "fruit inventory" and pray over one another.

Week 6: Chapter 5 — The Spirit Upon

- Focus: Power for witness, gifts, boldness.
- Discussion: Why did the disciples have to wait for the Spirit if they already believed?
- Activation: Create an "Upper Room" moment—pray, worship, and wait together for fresh filling.

Week 7: Chapter 6 — Grieve or Quench?

- Focus: How sin and resistance block flow.
- Discussion: What are common "leaks" in your walk?
- Activation: Use the repentance liturgy together as a group.

Weeks 8–10: Part III — Hosting the Presence (Chs. 7–10

Week 8: Chapter 7 — The Greenhouse Home

- Focus: Consecrating homes as dwelling places for God.

- Discussion: What atmosphere do people feel when they enter your home?
- Activation: Do a symbolic dedication of your group's meeting space.

Week 9: Chapter 8–9 — Holy Habits & Hearing and Obeying

- Focus: Rhythms of abiding + obedience to God's voice.
- Discussion: Share a time when a simple "yes" to God changed everything.
- Activation: Try the "90-second obedience" challenge during the week; report back.

Week 10: Chapter 10 — Clean Hands, Pure Heart

- Focus: Purity sustains power.
- Discussion: Why does righteousness matter for carrying authority?
- Activation: Communion together with a focus on holiness.

Weeks 11–12: Part IV — Demonstration (Chs. 11–15)

Week 11: Chapters 11–13 — Healing, Deliverance, Prophecy

- Focus: Demonstrating the kingdom in love and power.
- Discussion: Which of these three areas excites or intimidates you most?
- Activation: Pair up and pray for healing or encouragement words.

Week 12: Chapters 14–15 + Conclusion — Boldness & the Great Co-Mission

- Focus: Tongues, boldness, and disciple-making.
- Discussion: How will you multiply what you've received?
- Activation: Create personal Oikos Maps and pray over them as a group.

Leader's Notes

- Guard the culture. This is not about performance— it's about presence. Always create a safe environment of love and encouragement.
- Expect testimonies. Celebrate even small breakthroughs (a whisper heard, a partial healing, a small act of obedience).
- Keep Jesus central. Every gift, sign, or practice must point to Him, not just the experience.
- Multiply. Challenge participants to lead their own group after finishing.

APPENDIX E
SCRIPTURE INDEX & CONFESSION DECLARATIONS

"Death and life are in the power of the tongue, and those who love it will eat its fruit." — *Proverbs 18:21 NKJV*

The Word of God is a sword in your mouth. When you declare Scripture with faith, you agree with heaven's reality and invite it to manifest on earth. Below are categorized declarations with Scripture references, followed by sample confessions you can speak aloud.

1. Identity Confessions

Who you are in Christ.
Key Scriptures:

- John 1:12 — I am a child of God.
- 2 Corinthians 5:17 — I am a new creation.
- Ephesians 1:5 — I am adopted through Christ.
- Romans 8:1 — I am free from condemnation.

Declarations:

- I am a beloved child of God, chosen and adopted in Christ.
- My old life is gone; the new has come.
- There is no condemnation over me; I walk in freedom.
- I live with heaven's DNA, because Christ lives in me.

2. Authority Confessions

What you carry as a believer.
Key Scriptures:

- Luke 10:19 — I have authority to trample on snakes and scorpions.
- Matthew 28:18–20 — I am sent with Christ's authority.
- Mark 16:17–18 — Signs follow me as a believer.
- 1 John 4:4 — Greater is He in me than he who is in the world.

Declarations:

- I carry kingdom authority as a son/daughter of the King.
- In Jesus' name, I have power over darkness and freedom from fear.
- The Spirit within me is greater than any opposition outside of me.
- Wherever I go, the kingdom of God advances.

3. Holiness Confessions

Living consecrated and pure.
Key Scriptures:

- Psalm 24:3–4 — Clean hands and a pure heart ascend the hill of the Lord.
- 2 Timothy 2:21 — Vessels for honor are prepared for every good work.
- Galatians 5:22–23 — The Spirit produces fruit in me.
- 1 Peter 1:16 — Be holy as He is holy.

Declarations:

- My life is consecrated to God; I am His dwelling place.
- I walk with clean hands and a pure heart, sustained by His grace.
- The fruit of the Spirit grows in me daily: love, joy, peace, patience, kindness, goodness, faithfulness, gentleness, and self-control.
- Holiness is not a burden; it is the joy of living close to God.

4. Assignment Confessions

Your calling and mission.
Key Scriptures:

- Acts 1:8 — I am clothed with power to be a witness.
- Matthew 10:7–8 — I proclaim the kingdom and heal the sick.
- John 15:16 — I am chosen and appointed to bear lasting fruit.
- 2 Corinthians 5:20 — I am an ambassador for Christ.

Declarations:

- I am empowered to make disciples of all nations.

- My words and actions release the kingdom wherever I go.
- I am chosen and appointed by Jesus to bear fruit that remains.
- I represent heaven on earth as an ambassador of Christ.

5. Protection Confessions

God's covering over your life, family, and home.
Key Scriptures:

- Psalm 91:1–2 — I dwell in the shelter of the Most High.
- Numbers 6:24–26 — The Lord blesses and keeps me.
- 2 Thessalonians 3:3 — The Lord is faithful; He strengthens and protects me.
- Isaiah 54:17 — No weapon formed against me will prosper.

Declarations:

- I dwell in the shadow of the Almighty; His presence is my refuge.
- The Lord blesses and keeps me; His face shines upon me with peace.
- No weapon formed against me will prosper; every assignment of the enemy is broken.
- My home, my marriage, my children, and my future are covered in the blood of Jesus.

Daily Use Pattern
Here's a rhythm you can follow in 5 minutes a day:

1. Choose 1 category (Identity, Authority, Holiness, Assignment, Protection).
2. Read 2–3 Scriptures aloud.
3. Pray the Declarations out loud with conviction.
4. Pause & listen—often the Spirit will highlight one phrase or truth for you to carry that day.

APPENDIX F
TESTIMONY JOURNAL PAGES

"They overcame him by the blood of the Lamb and by the word of their testimony." — *Revelation 12:11 NIV*

A testimony is not just a memory—it's a prophecy of what God will do again. When we write down what God has done, we honor His work, strengthen our own faith, and release courage for others. Every testimony is seed for multiplication.

Why Record Testimonies?

1. Memory: We often forget what God has done; writing anchors it.
2. Faith: Reviewing past testimonies builds confidence for present battles.
3. Legacy: Your children and disciples need to know what God has done in your life.
4. Witness: Sharing your testimony is one of the simplest and most powerful evangelism tools.

Testimony Journal Template

Each testimony entry should capture both the story and the significance.

1. Date & Place

- When and where did it happen?

2. Who Was Involved?

- Names of people present (especially those prayed for or who witnessed the event).

3. The Need / Problem

- What was the situation before prayer or breakthrough?
- Example: sickness, oppression, financial need, salvation.

4. The Prayer / Action

- What step of faith was taken?
- Example: a prayer for healing, a prophetic word, a simple act of obedience.

5. The Breakthrough

- What did God do?
- Describe clearly: healed, delivered, provided, encouraged, etc.

6. The Impact

- How did this change the person's life?

- Was faith strengthened? Was Jesus glorified?

7. Scripture Anchor

- What verse connects to this testimony?
- Example: *"By His stripes we are healed" (Isaiah 53:5).*

8. My Reflection

- What did I learn about God's nature through this?
- What does this testimony mean for my life going forward?

9. Next Step / Prophecy

- How does this testimony shape my expectation?
- Write a short declaration: "God healed me then, He will heal again."

Sample Testimony Entry

Date & Place: March 5, 2025 — Tacoma Campus
Who Was Involved: Tom, prayer team, woman named Sarah
The Need: Sarah had chronic migraines for 10 years, daily pain.
The Prayer: Two of us laid hands on her head, commanded healing in Jesus' name.
The Breakthrough: Pain lifted instantly; she testified she felt "light" for the first time.
The Impact: She wept, family members shocked, faith stirred in the room.
Scripture Anchor: *Psalm 103:3 — "He heals all your diseases."*

My Reflection: God cares about long-term suffering; He restores joy and dignity.

Next Step: I will expect migraines to be healed wherever I minister.

Prompts for Sharing Testimonies in Groups

- "Where did you see God move this week?"
- "What prayer was answered recently?"
- "How did you experience His presence in your home, work, or city?"

Encourage short, 2–3 minute testimonies. Write them down afterward.

Monthly Review Section

At the end of each month, add a page:

- List your top 5 testimonies.
- Highlight recurring themes (healing, provision, salvation, inner healing).
- Pray: "Lord, do it again—and even greater."

Year-End Testimony Celebration

Take time at the end of the year to gather as a family, small group, or church.

- Read testimonies aloud.
- Give thanks for God's works.
- Create a "Memorial Wall" or digital timeline of His faithfulness.

ABOUT THE AUTHOR

Tom Cornell is the Senior Leader of SOZO Church in Washington state, founder of Walk in the Light International and SOZO Network. Tom is married to his beautiful wife Katy and lives in the Puget Sound area with her and their three kids. He has been in ministry pastoring and teaching the body of Christ since 2008.

He has a passion to see the body of Christ moving from people with an orphan mindset to that of sonship; equipping the body to do the work of Jesus resulting in seeing the Kingdom of God manifested here on earth.

www.ingramcontent.com/pod-product-compliance
Lightning Source LLC
LaVergne TN
LVHW052024080426
835513LV00018B/2154